a Simple Guide to

Excel 2000

Linda Steven

Prentice
Hall

An imprint of PEARSON EDUCATION

PEARSON EDUCATION LIMITED

Head Office:
Edinburgh Gate
Harlow
Essex CM20 2JE
Tel: +44 (0) 1279 623623
Fax: +44 (0) 1279 431059

London Office:
128 Long Acre
London WC2E 9AN
Tel: +44 (0) 171 447 2000
Fax: +44 (0) 171 240 5771

First published in Great Britain 2000

© Pearson Education Limited 2000

First published in 1999 as
Se Former En Un Jour: Excel 2000
by CampusPress France
19, rue Michel Le Comte
75003 Paris
France

Library of Congress Cataloging in Publication Data
Available from the publisher.

British Library Cataloguing in Publication Data
A CIP catalogue record for this book can be obtained from the British Library.

ISBN 0-13-016870-X

10 9 8 7 6 5 4 3 2 1

Translated and typeset by Cybertechnics, Sheffield.
Printed and bound in Great Britain by Ashford Colour Press, Gosport, Hampshire.

The publishers' policy is to use paper manufactured from sustainable forests.

Contents

....

Introduction

Excel 2000 is an improvement on Excel 97, but, it is claimed, will finally come into its own with Windows 2000, or so they say. There have been minor changes mainly aimed at making it easier to use. The only major new feature is the introduction of the euro. But there are also some other very interesting new features, such as: a 12-level clipboard, the ability to publish on the Web and some other sophisticated functions. And also:

- Improved opening and saving functions. It is easier to access files which have been previously opened. The memory retains the last 50 documents to be opened.

- Automatic fill displays lists of suggestions.

- Legends for charts have been improved. When there are long numbers, these are shortened for greater clarity.

- Macros are certified with a digital signature to improve security. This allows interception of viruses contained in files attached to e-mail messages.

- Four-figure dates are proposed as an option.

- It is possible to create Excel 2000 documents specifically for the Web. Tables become interactive on the Internet, up to a point.

- If there are coloured cells, the colour is not reversed on selection, which makes them more readable.

- Presentation of documents stored on the Internet has additional features usually not available on the Web. These can therefore be interpreted by Office 2000.

- PivotTables are better integrated and more powerful.

Excel 97 came with some major modifications, while the main point about Excel 2000 is that it is now part of Office 2000, a coherent and powerful suite of applications. It is a version which is in some way aimed at creating harmonisation between the various applications. Therefore, for users who upgrade from Excel 95 to Excel 2000, we will list here some of the enhancements which were present in Excel 97 and which are now part of Excel 2000.

■ Enhancements

Cells

Cells can contain 32,000 characters as opposed to the previous 255.

Worksheets

Worksheets contain 65,000 rows instead of the 16,000 in the 95 version. The syntax for calculations is much simplified.

Formatting and layout

With the WordArt design tools, Excel becomes the prince of layouts. Customised borders for tables or raised headers give the worksheet a totally new look. Automatic shapes, arrows, legends, symbols and other balloons substantially enhance the graphic environment. Excel 2000 also has access to the design tools available in Office 2000, which are in fact available for the whole suite of applications. For example, you can modify the level of depth of a composite object.

The Chart Wizard

The Chart Wizard is extremely easy to use. In four steps, the user can create high quality charts. To modify a chart, you can select each component with only one click. The layout of a 3D chart with textures and embedded images considerably improves the presentation value.

There are 63 types of charts available.

Sharing an Excel workbook
If you are networked, you can share a workbook and its worksheets. You can actually carry out multi-user modifications to your documents.

Internet
From within an Excel cell, you interrogate a site and retrieve data. You can access your e-mail and the whole network. The Internet will immediately recognise the Internet address when you enter it.

In addition, you can save your work directly on the Internet site of your choice. The remote server simply behaves in the same way as an additional hard disk.

Human, too human
The Office Assistants will guide you and will give you advice every step of the way. They bring a very human dimension to the interface, which in the previous version was perhaps a bit impersonal.

■ Symbols

Under this heading, you will find additional information.

This symbol warns you about problems you may encounter in certain cases. It also warns you what not to do. If you follow the instructions, you should not have any problems.

This symbol provides you with suggestions and tips: keyboard shortcuts, advanced techniques, and so on.

1
Discovering the software

Installing Excel 2000
Starting Excel 2000
Discovering the screen
Worksheets
Cells
Using a dialog box
Getting to know the Office Assistants

Excel 2000 opens a larger window on the Internet, a platform of macros compatible with Microsoft Word 2000, thanks to the new version of Visual Basic for applications, and some astonishing graphic improvements.

■ Installing Excel 2000

Before using the functions available in Excel 2000, it is advisable to become familiar with the interface for which this accounting package is famous.

What you need for configuring Excel 2000

To be able to install and use Excel 2000, you will need:

- A 486 or Pentium PC.
- Windows 95 or later, or Windows NT. Windows 2000 is recommended.
- A minimum RAM of 8 MB.
- A hard disk with approximately 100 MB free disk space for a complete installation.
- A CD-ROM reader.
- A Windows-compatible screen.
- A Microsoft-compatible mouse.

Installing Excel 2000

To install Excel 2000, do the following:

1. Switch on your computer and start Windows.
2. Insert the CD-ROM called 'Excel 2000' or 'Office 2000' into your drive.
3. Click the Install button.
4. From now on, you are guided by various messages displayed in the installation program dialog boxes.

■ Starting Excel 2000

To start Excel 2000:

1. Click the Start button in the Taskbar.

2. Click the Microsoft Excel option.

The Excel program is now launched. The default worksheet 1 of workbook 1 is displayed.

■ Discovering the screen

The Excel screen is where you will be working. You need to discover it first, and then customise it. Remember that you can actually choose the toolbars you wish to display and even the items on the bars. Excel is a nifty piece of software, if you take the trouble to get to know it properly.

The Excel window

In the top right hand corner of the screen, there is a button called Restore Window. This allows you to toggle between full screen display and a display in a window.

If you click on this, the worksheet will be displayed in a window.

The Maximize icon will bring the display back to full screen.

The black cross icon, located next to the Maximize and Restore Window icons, closes the window.

The Title bar

This is located at the top of the window. It indicates the name of the application, 'Microsoft Excel'.

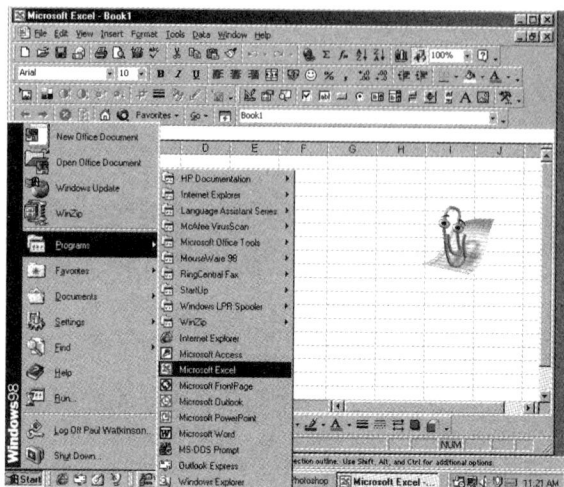

Figure 1.1 The Start button in the Taskbar and the Microsoft Excel 2000 option.

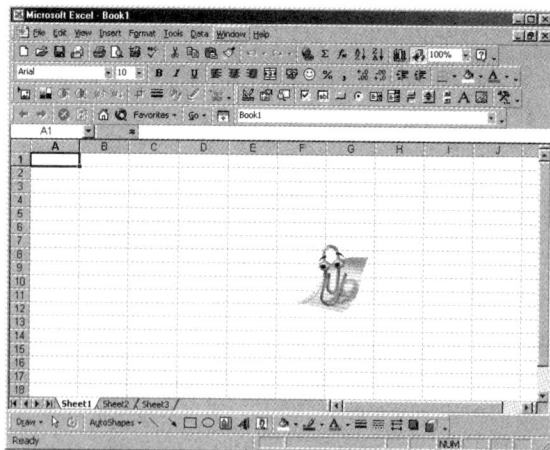

Figure 1.2 Worksheet 1 of workbook 1 is displayed as the default.

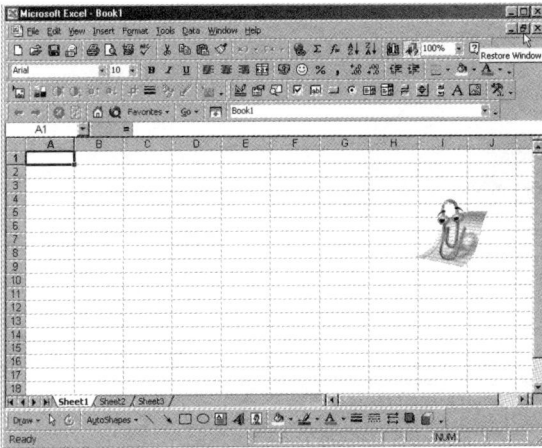

Figure 1.3 The Restore Window button resizes the window and brings it back to its original place.

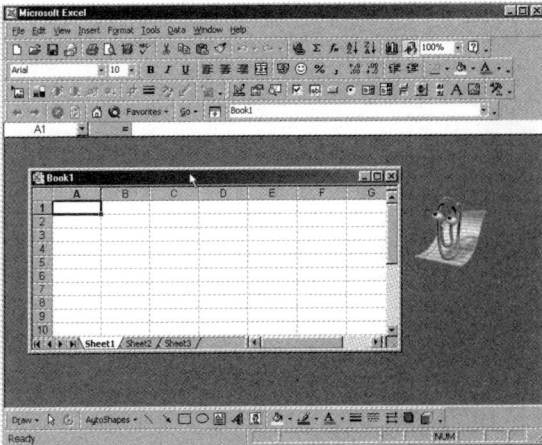

Figure 1.4 The worksheet will be displayed in a window.

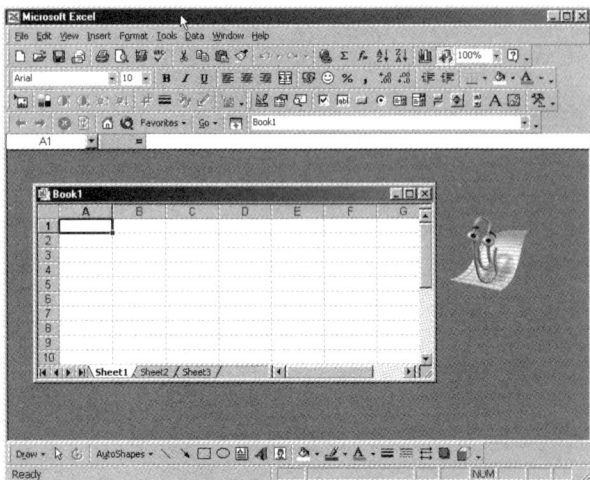

Figure 1.5 The Title bar.

The Menu bar

This is located under the Title bar. It lists the name of the 9 drop-down menus.

Figure 1.6 The Menu bar.

The Toolbar

Excel offers nine default Toolbars. It allows their complete customisation and the creation of additional bars. These bars can be freely moved.

Two default Toolbars are displayed: Standard and Layout.

Figure 1.7 The Standard and Layout toolbars.

Hiding a Toolbar

You can hide a Toolbar whenever you want.

With the right-hand mouse button:

1. Click any Toolbar.
2. In the context menu displayed, click the Toolbar you wish to display or hide.

The Status bar

The Status bar is located at the bottom of the screen. It can be removed if you wish to enlarge the worksheet. On its left side, it provides information about the mode you are working in, as well as about the activation of some keys on the keyboard.

The Formula bar

The Formula bar allows you to view and modify the contents of the cells in your worksheet. It shows the data you are entering into the cell. When it is active, the Cancel and Enter icons are displayed.

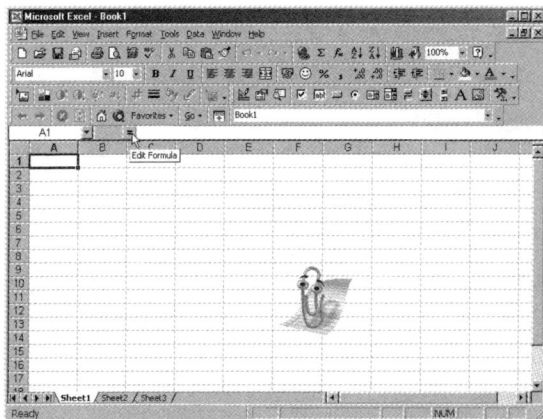

Figure 1.8 The Formula bar.

The Name box

The Name box, located under the toolbar, and to the left, indicates the references for the active cell; for example, 'C9', if the active cell is C9.

ScreenTips

If you position and hold your cursor on a button for a few seconds, the function of the button will be explained in ScreenTip. It is an extremely useful reminder. To deactivate ScreenTips:

1. Open the View menu.
2. Select the Toolbars submenu.
3. Choose the Customize option.
4. Click on the Options tab.

You can also use this reminder by opening the Help pull-down menu, then selecting 'What's This?' and placing the resulting ? onto a button of your choice or an item in the window to obtain its description.

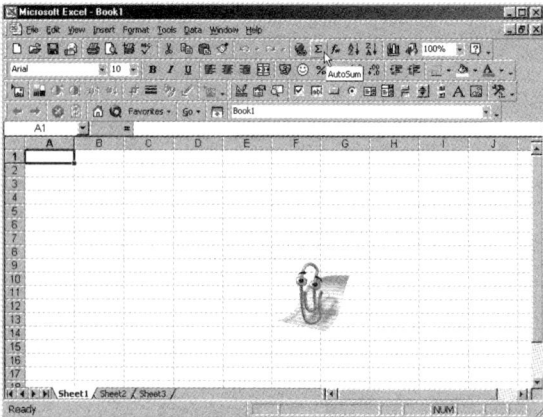

Figure 1.9 The explanation 'AutoSum' will appear in the ScreenTip.

Vertical and horizontal scroll bars

The scroll bars and the scrolling arrows allow you to move quickly to view other sections in the worksheet.

To scroll through a worksheet, you have two methods, according to whether you are using the mouse or the keyboard. The scroll bars are used with the mouse.

To scroll through a column or a row, click the arrow which points to where you wish to scroll, at the edge of the horizontal or vertical scroll bars.

Let us assume that you wish to move one column to its right. Your screen shows columns A to G. To fill a cell in column H, simply click on the black arrow pointing to the right of the horizontal scroll bar.

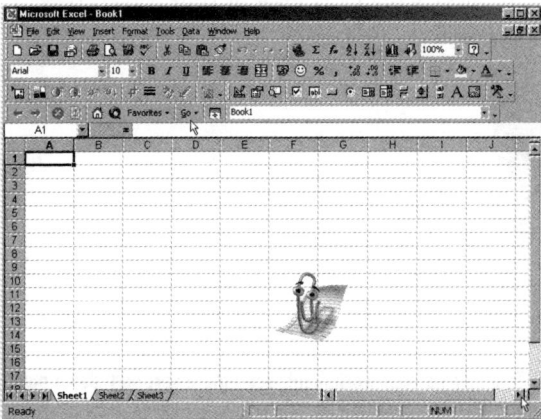

Figure 1.10 The horizontal scroll bar.

■ Worksheets

A worksheet contains over 4 million cells arranged on 256 columns and 65,536 rows. The worksheet is always stored in a workbook. The screen will only show you a small part of your worksheet.

A workbook includes several worksheets. Excel currently has three default worksheets, but you can always add more whenever you wish.

1. Open the Insert menu.
2. Click the Worksheet option.
3. Confirm.

You had three worksheets displayed on the screen; now you have four. To display the worksheet of your choice, select its tab.

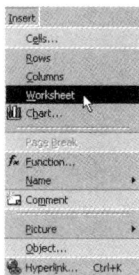

Figure 1.11 To display a new worksheet, open the Insert pull-down menu and click on the Worksheet option.

Moving within the worksheet with the keyboard

To move between cells on the worksheet with the keyboard, you have seven arrow keys, specific keys and the combination of these keys with the arrows:

- **Upwards pointing arrow:** move one cell up.
- **Downwards pointing arrow:** move one cell down.
- **Left pointing arrow:** move one cell left.
- **Right pointing arrow:** move one cell right.
- **Home:** moves to the first cell in the active row.
- **Upward arrow crossed with three small horizontal lines, called 'Page up' (PgUp):** move up one screen.
- **Downward arrow crossed with three small horizontal lines, called 'Page down' (PgDn):** move down one screen.
- **Ctrl+PgDn:** move to the next sheet in the workbook.
- **Ctrl+PgUp:** move to the previous sheet in the workbook.
- **Ctrl+Right arrow:** move to the cell just to the right which is not empty or to the last cell in the row.
- **Ctrl+Left arrow:** move to the cell just to the left which is not empty or to the first cell in the row.
- **Ctrl+Down arrow:** move to the cell just below which is not empty or to the first cell in the column.
- **Ctrl+Up arrow:** move to the cell just above which is not empty or to the first cell in the column.
- **Ctrl+Home:** move to the first cell in the worksheet.
- **Ctrl+End:** move to the last cell in the worksheet, which is the cell at the intersection of the furthest right used column and the bottom most used row (in the lower right-hand corner), or the cell opposite the home cell, which is typically A1.

■ Cells

The cell is the primary element in Excel. It can contain different types of data: number, text, formula, and so on.

The active cell is surrounded by a thicker border. This is the cell which will be affected by your next action.

Each cell has its own address, which corresponds to the combination of the row number and the column letter. The address can be absolute or relative. The relative address is the default working mode, because it makes copying formulas easier.

Selecting a cell with the mouse

To get into a cell, simply position the cursor shaped as a white cross on the cell you wish to make active and click.

■ Using a dialog box

Dialog boxes provide full and complete guidance and information as you work. They include several pages; to access them you simply click on tabs. A dialog box may contain:

- **Text boxes.** These are to be filled with a series of characters or numerical values, to be typed in on the keyboard.

- **Option buttons.** These contain additional orders for executing a command. These are activated or deactivated with a single click.

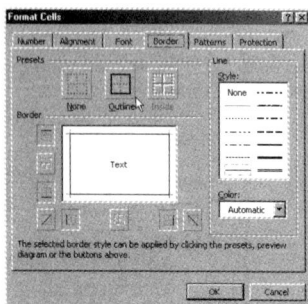

Figure 1.12 The Format Cells dialog box.

- **Selection boxes.** As opposed to the option buttons, in an option field you can only activate one selection. The active selection is marked with a black circle.

- **Click-on list boxes.** These contain a list of predefined possibilities, one of which is selected by default.

- **Buttons.** These are used to confirm or cancel your command. Some boxes also have additional buttons, which allow you to open additional dialog boxes.

- **Meters.** Meters are small boxes with arrows pointing upwards and downwards to allocate numerical values.

- **Close box.** The Close box is an icon in the shape of a cross. It is located in the top right-hand corner of the dialog box. If you click this, the dialog box will be closed.

■ Getting to know the Office Assistants

Excel 2000 provides you with eight Assistants whose task it is to guide you in understanding the application. The Office Assistant is an interactive program.

Each Assistant answers immediately any question you may have on how to carry out specific tasks. If you wish to call them up, click the little box with a question mark in the top right-hand corner of your screen.

In the dialog box which opens, specify what you would like to do. Once your question is clearly stated, you have a choice of two buttons:

- Search.
- Options.

If you type the name 'Office Assistant' and click the Search button, a little character known as Clippit will ask you if you want to show, hide or turn off the Office Assistant, get help without using the Assistant, turn the Assistant sound on or off, see more, and so on.

If you click on Options, the Gallery and Options are displayed. The Options tab offers various options to be selected, such as Respond to F1 key, Help with wizards, Make sounds or Move when in the way. The Gallery tab will introduce you to all the various Office Assistants.

Figure 1.13 The Microsoft Office portrait gallery.

The first Assistant, Clippit, will provide you with useful and comprehensive advice. When you have a precise question to ask, type the keyword in the text box (for example, 'Tabs'): Clippit will then suggest a list of operations connected to tabs. It is now up to you to select the one which would answer your question.

Let us assume, for example, that you wish to display additional sheet tabs. The Office Assistant will provide you with a new list of operations, which will take you through all the necessary steps for displaying additional sheet tabs.

To display additional sheet tabs, click this option in the list provided by the Assistant with the little hand, and you will get the answer.

These are the eight Office Assistants you will find in Excel:

■ Assistant 1: Clippit. General guidance.

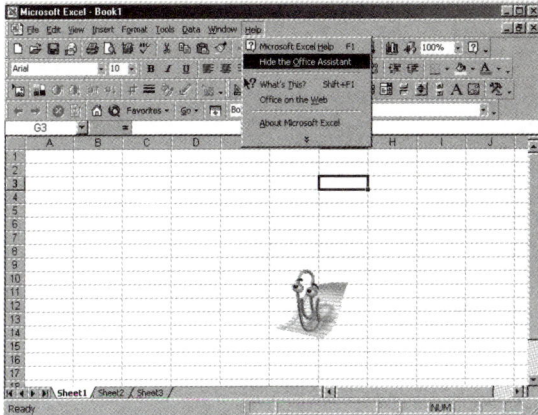

Figure 1.14 The Office Assistant button.

- Assistant 2: The Dot.
- Assistant 3: F1 is the first of the 300/M series, built to serve.
- Assistant 4: The Genius. He looks like Albert (Einstein, of course!).
- Assistant 5: Office Logo. It gives you help accompanied by a little spin of its coloured pieces...

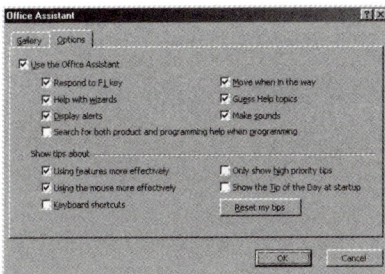

Figure 1.15 The Office Assistant dialog box.

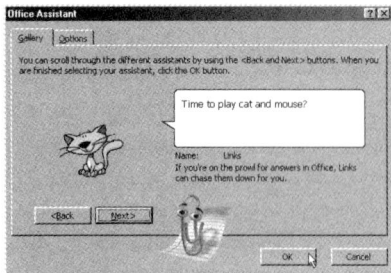

Figure 1.16 Select one of the eight Office Assistants.

- Assistant 6: Mother Nature. It spins.
- Assistant 7: Links. A cat which will not chase your mouse.
- Assistant 8: Rocky. A guide dog for computers.

Choose the one you like best!

2 Entering data

■ Opening a new workbook

When you launch the program, you have immediately available a default workbook called 'Book 1'. You can work in this workbook and give it a name later.

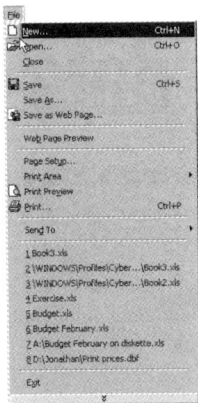

Figure 2.1 Select New in the File menu.

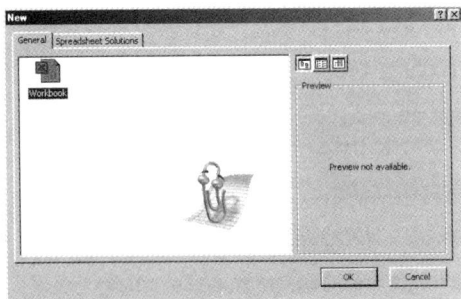

Figure 2.2 The new workbook dialog box.

To use a new workbook, open the File menu and select New. In the dialog box, click Workbook, then OK.

The workbook which appears has three default worksheets. The first one is the active worksheet.

■ Renaming the active worksheet

We are going to rename the active worksheet, Sheet1, Chapt._02. To do this, click with the right mouse button the tab of the active worksheet, at the bottom of the screen to the left. In the context menu which is displayed, click Rename. The cursor is placed on the tab to be renamed. All you need to do now is type the required text, in this case Chapt._02.

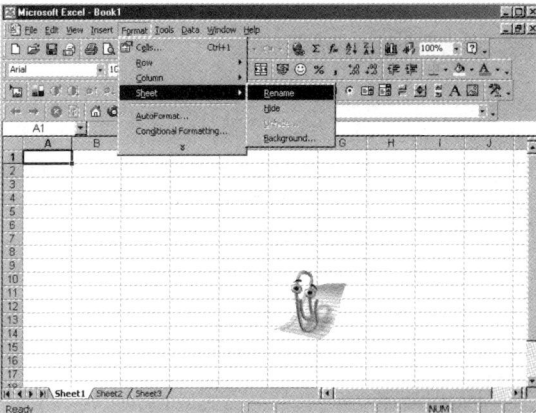

Figure 2.3 Renaming the active worksheet.

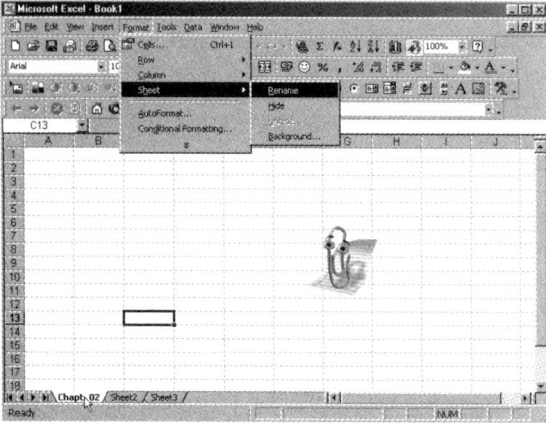

Figure 2.4 Type `Chapt._02` on the tab in your active worksheet.

■ Opening an existing workbook

To open an existing workbook, use the File menu, Open and select the workbook in the dialog box which is now displayed. You can also open one of these workbooks directly by opening the File menu, because Excel stores the last four most recently opened workbooks.

If you had given your workbook a password in the Save Options dialog box, you will need to enter it before being able to access your document.

Enter the data.

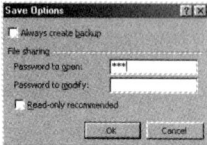

Figure 2.5 The password in the Save Options.

■ Entering data

Entering data in an area

You only need to select a group of connected or disconnected cells, and the range will receive information while you are entering data.

Data contained in the active cell, during or after the enter operation, are displayed in the Formula bar. To modify data, click the text displayed in this bar or use the F2 key.

Entering numbers

To enter a number, enter the first number; on occasions preceded by the + or – sign. The accepted characters are: ( ) / * and % E and F.

Entering date and time

Excel uses the calendar starting from 1900: the serial numbers correspond to dates between 1 January, 1900 and 31 December, 9999.

To modify the date system:

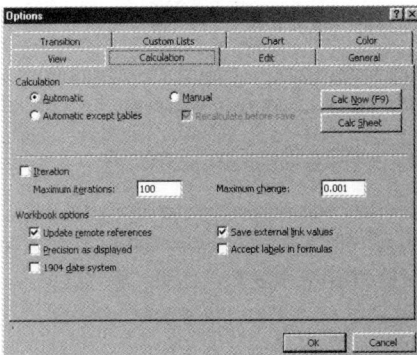

Figure 2.6 To modify the date system, select or deselect the 1904 date system box.

Figure 2.7 Enter 28/12/1999 into a cell. Then drag downwards as in the illustration. The date will now show the year 2000.

1. Open the Tools menu.
2. Select Options.
3. Click the Calculation tab.
4. Select or deselect the 1904 date system box.

Entering text

For Excel, anything which is not a number, a date, time or formula is text. A text can include figures, letters or symbols, but it cannot exceed 32,000 characters per cell.

If we want to see all the steps for entering text, let us take an example. Let us assume that you want to calculate the cost of preparing a French regional dish from Alsace, the Baeckhoffe (a sort of stew made with three types of meat).

In column A, you will enter the names of the ingredients; in column B, the required quantities; and in column C, the price for each ingredient.

1. Start by clicking cell C1.
2. Type the words Ingredients, Weight and Price in cells A1, B1 and C1. When you enter your text, this is displayed in

the Formula bar as you are typing it. If you make a mistake, use the Backspace key.

3. When you have typed Price, confirm your entries with Enter.

4. Click the next cell.

5. Once you have done the column headers, enter the recipe in columns, following the illustration.

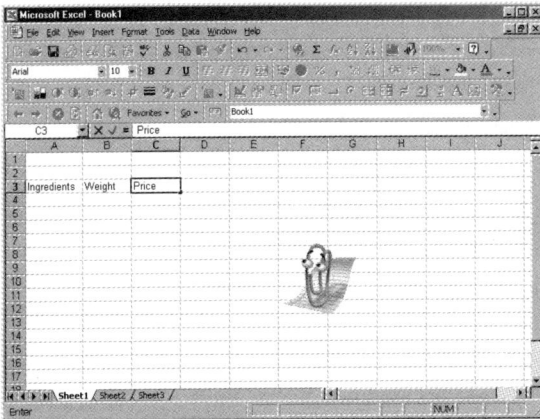

Figure 2.8 Entering data in the A, B and C columns.

Recipe for Baeckhoffe, or Alsatian stew, found on the Internet.

Marinade 500g of brisket of beef in Alsatian wine for 24 hours, as well as 500g of shoulder of lamb and 500g of shoulder of pork, all cut into pieces.

Put the meat in an earthenware bowl, on a layer of thinly sliced potatoes. Cover this with a layer of thinly sliced onions, a layer of potatoes and a second layer of onions. Sprinkle with some more Alsatian wine. Cook in the oven for approximately 2$\frac{1}{2}$ hours, then serve. You may want to serve it with a Pinot blanc, gris or noir.

When you type the text in column A, it spills over into column B; and when you enter the contents of column B, the overspilling text from column A is no longer visible: therefore you must adjust the width of the columns for a better looking presentation.

■ Using the currency style

When you wish to enter prices in your table, you can enter them as whole numbers, or as currency with or without decimal points for larger figures.

To access these different style:

1. Open the Format Menu.
2. Select Cells.
3. The Format Cells dialog box appears.
4. Choose the Number tab and then Currency in the Category list.

The currency styles are used for general currency values. If you wish to align decimal points, use the Accounting style in the column.

The Currency Style button applies the dollar sign to the selected cells. According to the country chosen in the Windows Regional Settings dialog box which you access from the Control Panel, the International Currency Style button is displayed instead of the Currency Style button.

■ Modifying column width

The simplest way to adjust the width of the A column is to place the mouse pointer on the line that joins column A to column B. The pointer now becomes a bi-directional arrow: click and drag the mouse until you have reached the required width.

The standard column width corresponds to the average of the numbers between 0 and 9 which can be contained in one cell according to the selected font. To adjust the column width to its contents, double click the border at the top right of the column.

If you assign a default width to columns, this will apply the same width to all columns, apart from those which had previously been modified.

■ Undo and Redo

With the keyboard

If you make a mistake, you do not have to live with it. Press and hold down the Ctrl key and then press Z (Ctrl+Z). This undoes your last action. If you use the same key combination again, you will undo the previous action, and so on sixteen times. To reinstate your entry, use the combination Ctrl+Y.

With the mouse

To undo a current action with the mouse, click the Standard toolbar button which is a blue arrow pointing to the left. The black arrow on its right displays a pull-down list with the last actions which can be undone.

The Redo button (the blue arrow pointing to the right) undoes the action carried out by the Undo command. The black arrow also opens a drop-down list containing the latest actions which can be redone.

■ Selecting cells

Cell selection is a basic operation when using the worksheet. It consists of highlighting several cells in order to apply a command to them.

You can select a range of cells, either adjacent or non-adjacent.

- **Adjacent cells.** Click the first cell of the range and then drag to the last cell.
- **Non-adjacent cells.** Select the first cell or range of cells, and then hold down Ctrl and select the other cells or ranges.
- **A single cell.** Click the cell or press the arrow key to move to the cell.
- **Row or column.** Click the row or column heading.
- **Whole sheet.** Click the Select All button, or use Ctrl+A.

There is another method for selecting the range of relevant cells on the sheet:

1. Click the topmost cell on the left of the sheet and keep the Shift key pressed.
2. At the same time, open the Edit menu and select Go To.
3. Click the Special button.
4. Select the Last cell option in the Select dialog box.
5. Confirm by clicking OK. You can now release the Shift key.

Once you have completed your sheet, you may wish to make the column headings bold. To do this, select the three relevant cells. Go to the first cell, cell A4. Click and drag to cell C4. Release the mouse button. The range of three cells has now been selected. The first remains empty, and the others are in reversed-out mode, which means they appear as black on a white background. Now simply click on the Bold button.

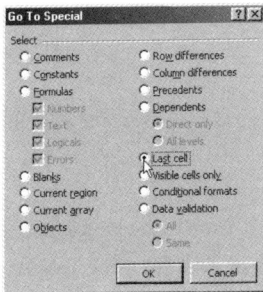

Figure 2.9 The Select dialog box allows you to go to the last relevant cell on the sheet, even if it is not closed.

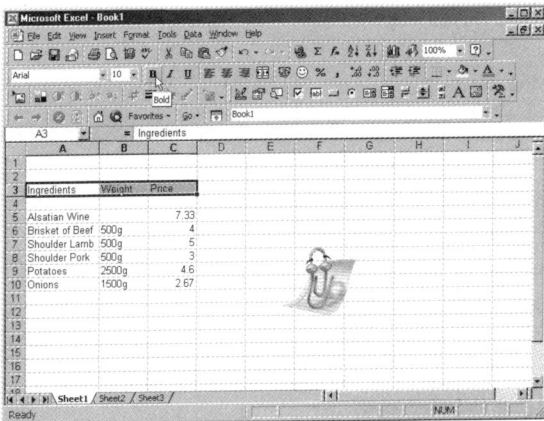

Figure 2.10 Select the Bold button to show your characters in bold.

■ Finding and replacing the contents of several cells

To find and replace the contents of several cells:

1. Select the range of cells in which you wish to make a replacement.

■■

2. Open the Edit menu, then click Replace.

3. In the Find what field, choose the text or the numbers you wish to replace.

4. In the Replace with Field, type what you wish to replace the previous entry with.

5. Click Find Next.

6. To replace data one at a time, click on Replace every time.

7. If you wish to replace everything in one go, click Replace All.

8. To cancel a current search, press Esc.

■ Clearing cells

1. Select the cells, the rows or the columns you wish to clear.

2. Open the Edit menu, click Clear. A submenu is displayed, which gives you the choice between various options:

- All.
- Formats.
- Contents.
- Comments.

■ Saving a workbook

When you have been working on your workbook for a while, you should save it on your hard disk. In this way there is no risk of losing your work.

Windows 95 uses the word Document to indicate data stored on disk, while Word, Excel and Access use the word File in menus.

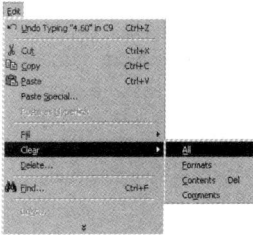

Figure 2.11 Select the Clear option and All to clear the whole contents of a cell.

To save:

1. Open the File menu.

2. Select Save or click on the button in the Toolbar which looks like a diskette.

3. Since your workbook does not have a name, Book1 is the default title. Replace this with a name of your choice, in this case Quicklearn.

4. Choose a directory and click Save.

Information on a workbook

The General tab provides information on the selected file. Open the File menu, select Properties, then click on the General tab.

■ Saving a workbook with a new name

You can change the name of your workbook and save it to another drive.

1. Open the File menu.

2. Select Save As. In the displayed dialog box, select the drive where you wish to save your workbook.

3. In the File name field, enter the new name.

Once your workbook has been named and saved, you only need to click the Save button to save any further changes.

Figure 2.12 shows this operation, with the C: drive, the directory, and, as the new name for your workbook, 'Book 2'.

Figure 2.12 Select the directory where you are saving your file and the new name for your workbook.

■ Saving a workbook with its properties

To save a workbook with its properties:

1. Open the File menu.
2. Select Properties.
3. Click the Summary tab.
4. Fill the text boxes Title, Subject, and so on.
5. If necessary, add some comments.
6. Confirm with OK.

You can have Excel 2000 create a backup copy of your file when saving. This operation allows you to keep the previous version, with the .BAK suffix. Open the File menu, click Save As, then on the General Options button in Tools and choose Always create backup copy.

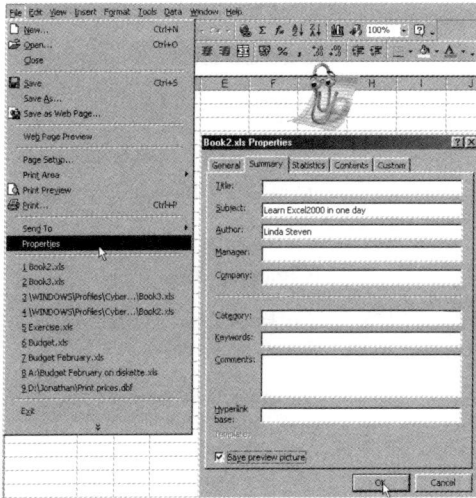

Figure 2.13 **The properties for your workbook saved in the Summary tab of the Properties dialog box. Some boxes must be filled by you.**

■ Changing a file format

To simplify sharing a worksheet with other software or computers (Macs, for example), you can choose the file format when saving it.

1. Open the File menu.

2. Select Save As.

3. In the File name box, select the file format you require.

The main file types

The following are the main file types:

Microsoft Excel	Workbook (extension .XLS).
Microsoft Excel 97/2000	Workbook (extension .XLS).
Microsoft Excel 95	Workbook (extension .XLS).
Web Page	(extension .htm or .html).
Template	(extension .XLT).
Text	(Tab delimited; extension .txt.
CSV	(Comma delimited; extension .csv).
Unicode Text	(extension .txt)
Microsoft Excel 5.0/95	Workbook old version of Excel.
SYLK	Symbolic link or Excel versions before v1.5.
Text (MS-DOS)	For text handling, spacing or tabs.
WKS WKI	For Lotus.
Mac	For Mac.

Obviously, at the moment you want Microsoft Excel Workbook with the extension .XLS.

3 Formatting

■ Drag and drop

Before looking at the tools available in Excel to format your work area, you should learn how to move one or more cells with the drag and drop method.

1. Select the C10:A1 area, which is your whole working area.

2. Place your pointer on the edge of the selected area. The pointer becomes a white arrow.

3. Press and hold the mouse button.

4. Drag the pointer to a new position, for example the B6:D15 area. Whilst you are moving it, the selection border becomes dark gray.

5. Release the mouse button. If you release it too early, your area may be in the wrong position. Simply click the Undo button in the toolbar or press Ctrl+Z to cancel the operation.

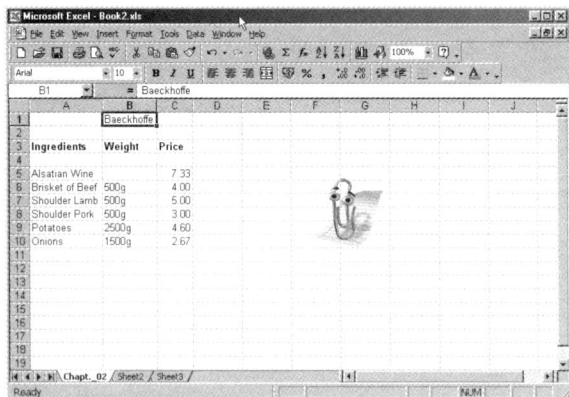

Figure 3.1 Before formatting your worksheet, choose its title.

■ Entering a title for your worksheet

To give your worksheet a name:

1. Place the pointer at the intersection of row 1 with column B, which is in cell B1.
2. Click. The selection marker appears around the cell.
3. Choose the title `Baeckhoffe`.
4. Confirm by pressing the Enter key.

■ Aligning a title

You note that your title is left-aligned on cell C6. Excel aligns text to the left of the cell. The default time, dates and numbers are right-aligned. You can modify the alignment and choose one of the options in the Format toolbar:

- **Align Left.** Left-align selected text, numbers or embedded objects.
- **Align Right.** Right-align selected text, numbers or embedded objects.
- **Center.** Centre selected text, numbers or embedded objects.

Select the title you have chosen. Click the Center button in the Format toolbar. You can repeat the same operation for other data in the sheet, for example for subtitles.

■ Merging and centring cells

The Merge and Center button combines two or more adjacent selected cells into one. The resulting merged cell only contains data placed in the top left-hand corner of the selection, which appear as centred in the new cell.

To centre a title over several columns, you must start by selecting the columns across which you wish to centre your title. Let us assume that you wish to centre your title 'Baeckhoffe' across all the columns in your sheet. To do this, select the B6:D6 area and click on the Merge and Center button.

Your title is now centred across columns B, C and D.

■ Changing size and font

With Windows 95, you use True Type fonts. The advantage is that their screen representation is identical to the printing fonts, and can be reproduced by any printer. The True Type label is indicated by a double T next to each font.

The default font, Times New Roman, gives a standard presentation. It is applied to new documents created from the active template.

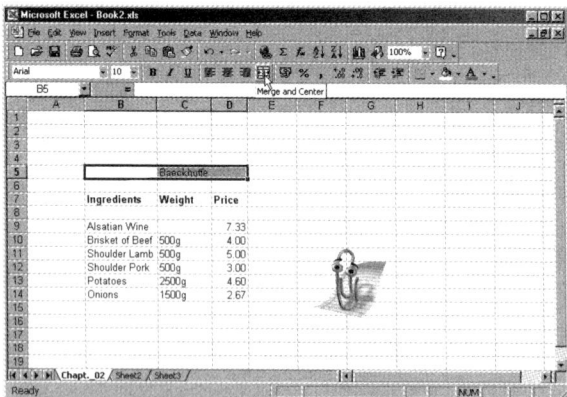

Figure 3.2 Merging cells for a worksheet title.

Changing font

Let us assume that the you are happy with the font you are using.

1. Select your work area, in this case area B6:D15.
2. Open the Format menu.
3. Click the Cell option.
4. Select the Font tab.
5. Click the Bodoni font.

The font used in your sheet is now Bodoni with size 11.

Changing font size

If the characters in your sheet are too big, choose a smaller font size.

1. Select all your work area, which is the B6:D14 area.
2. Open the menu Format.
3. Select the Cells option.
4. Click the Font tab.
5. Choose size 11 of the Bodoni font, which is what your worksheet is currently using.

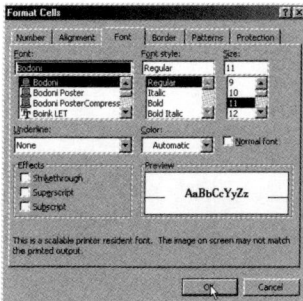

Figure 3.3 Changing font and size for characters.

■ Modifying a row height

You can use two different techniques to modify the height of a row.

With the interface

The edges of the horizontal rows which separate cells can be moved. After you have selected the cell area for which you wish to modify the height, position your pointer on the edge of a horizontal row. The pointer now changes to a vertical double black arrow. Let us assume that the height of the cells with the subtitles of your sheet is insufficient.

1. Select the A8:D8 area.

2. Place your pointer at the beginning of the row.

3. Adjust the height of the row as you want it. Let us assume that you no longer want the standard height 12, but the height 17.75.

4. Press and hold the left mouse button, after selecting page 8.

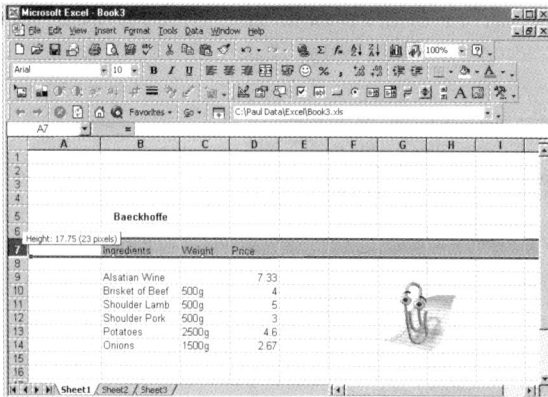

Figure 3.4 Modifying the height of a row in the work area with the interface.

5. Drag the pointer 'Vertical double arrow' downwards, until you achieve the right size, to increase the row height.

With the Format menu

1. Select the subtitles area B8:D8.
2. Open the Format menu.
3. Select the submenu row.
4. Click on the Height option.
5. In the dialog box type the value you wish to assign to your row height: 17.75.

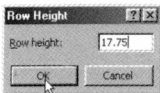

Figure 3.5 Modifying the height of a row in your work area with the Format menu.

■ Modifying a column width

The column heading separators can be moved at will. Click on the separating line in the column headings B and C. Your pointer now becomes a bi-directional arrow. Drag to the right until you reach the value you want, say 16.14.

■ Orienting text

Inside a cell, text can be rotated by up to 90°. You can rotate your text clockwise or anti-clockwise.

1. Select the subtitles in your menu.
2. Open the Format menu.
3. Click the Cell submenu.

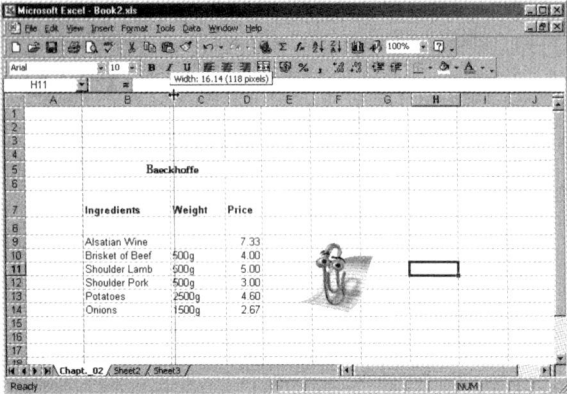

Figure 3.6 Modifying a column width with the interface.

4. Click the Alignment tab.

5. Choose the Orientation option.

6. Select value 7 in the Degrees box.

Your subtitles are rotated by 7° – but it does not look that good! It is up to you to choose the best possible orientation for the message you wish to convey.

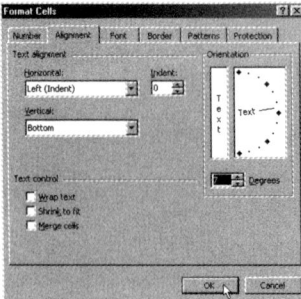

Figure 3.7 Rotating your subtitles by 7° from lower left to upper right.

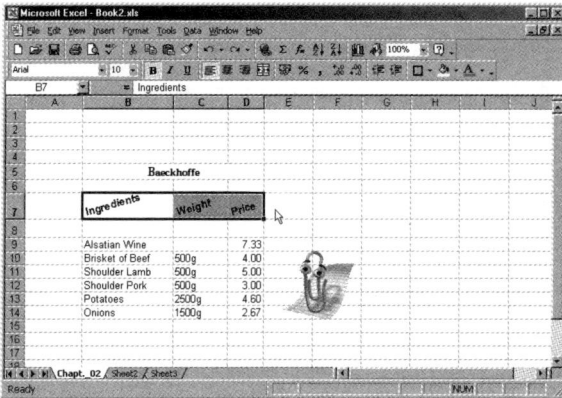

Figure 3.8 A very optimistic chart!

The orientation of the text may well conflict with other presentation features, for example, with the alignment. In this case, you will have to make a choice.

If you have saved a workbook in a different file format, the text rotation effect may be lost. Most file formats cannot cope with total rotation to 180° (from + 90° to – 90°) which is allowed by Excel 2000. Previous Excel versions accept a + 90° text rotation, from 0° (zero) or from – 90°. If the specified rotation angle is not maintained in a different file format, the text is not rotated.

■ Fitting text

Let us assume this time that your subtitles are much larger than the cell.

1. Open the Format menu.
2. Click the Cell submenu.

3. Click the Alignment option.

4. Tick the Shrink to fit box.

Your title now fits the width available in the cell.

■ Adding a border

With the interface
To add a border with the interface:

1. Select your work area.

2. Click the arrow next to the Borders button. This will change the appearance of the button.

3. Click the type of border you require.

Your work area now has a border.

With the menu
Whenever you want, you can change the look and thickness of your border, if you do not like the one you have chosen.

1. Select your work area.

2. Open the Format menu.

3. Select the Cell submenu.

4. Click the Border tab.

5. Select an option under Style to specify the line size and style for a border.

6. Confirm with OK.

Your work area now has a customised border.

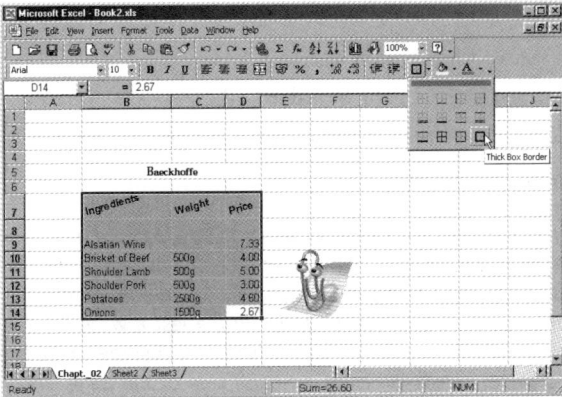

Figure 3.9 Adding a border with the Borders button.

Modifying the colour of a row or the border around a drawing object

1. Select the object you wish to modify.
2. In the Draw toolbar, click the arrow next to Line Color.
3. Click the colour you wish to apply.

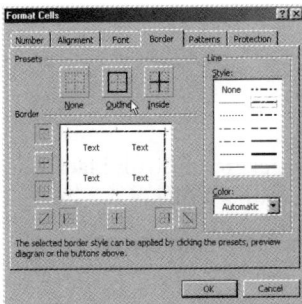

Figure 3.10 Adding a border to your work area with the menu.

If the colour you want is not displayed:

1. Click More Line Colors.
2. Click one colour, in the Standard tab.
3. Click the Customize tab to create a customised colour.
4. Confirm by clicking OK.

If you wish to print the same border for cells separated by a page break, so that the border appears only on one page, use the Cell command in the Format menu to apply an internal border. For example, to print a border underneath the last row on a page, and to show the same border at the top of the first row in the following page, select the rows on each side of the page break, then click Cell, in the Format menu. Click the Border tab, then the Inside button under Presets. Under Border, deactivate the vertical border by clicking it in the record shown.

■ Adding patterns

If you want to achieve even better looking results, you can add patterns to your cells:

1. Select the area of cells B6:D6 which have your title 'Baeckhoffe'.
2. Open the Format menu.
3. Select the Cell submenu.
4. Click the Patterns tab.
5. Click the Patterns palette.
6. Select a pattern with a white background with black dots which gives a grey impression with a value of 6.25%.

Your work area is getting to look better and better!

Adding background patterns to your worksheet

To add a background pattern to your worksheet:

1. Click the area on the worksheet where you wish to add a background pattern.

2. Open the Format menu.

3. Click Sheet.

4. Click Background.

5. Select the picture files you want to use for the background pattern.

The selected picture is then reproduced over the whole worksheet. You can apply Fill effects to cells containing data.

If the Background command is not available, make sure that you have selected only one worksheet.

■ Shading a cell

To emphasise the subtitles, you can, for example, shade cells.

1. Select your area B8:D8.

2. Open the Format menu.

3. Select the Cell submenu.

4. Click the Patterns tab.

5. Click one colour in the Cell shading option.

■ Automatic formatting

To create a layout for a whole list or a large area which includes separate elements, such as column and row labels, summary totals or detailed data, you can apply a predefined

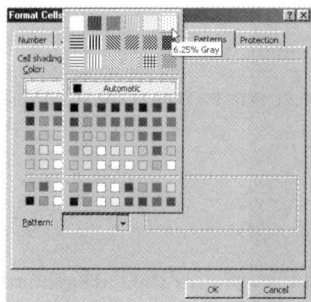

Figure 3.11 Selecting a pattern.

sheet template known as 'AutoFormat'. This template uses different formats according to the nature of the elements in the sheet.

To apply several formats at a time and to guarantee that the cells have a coherent layout, you can apply a style to them.

If you think that your presentation could be even more attractive, use an automatic layout.

1. Select your work area.
2. Open the Format menu.
3. Click the AutoFormat option. The dialog box now displays 17 different types of automatic layout for your sheet.
4. Choose List 2.

Copying layout from one cell area to another

To copy the layout from one cell area to another, you can use the Copy button in the Standard toolbar. This function allows you to copy the layout of the selected object, then apply this to the object or text on which you click.

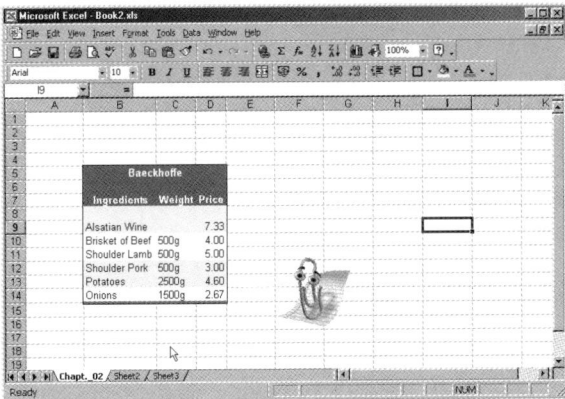

Figure 3.12 Your work area now has an automatic layout and has acquired a truly professional look!

To copy the layout for several elements, double-click Copy, then click each element for which you wish to create the layout. When finished, press Esc or click again.

4
WordArt

▪▪▪

WordArt allows you to create contrasts within documents for a pleasing presentation that can satisfy everybody. Don't overdo it, but whatever you do, do it properly. This chapter will be dedicated to the pleasures of producing graphic objects with the various tools at your disposal, which makes this a creative exercise.

▪ Drawing graphic objects

The AutoShapes menu in the Drawing toolbar contains several predefined drawing categories. In total, there is a choice of 100 AutoShapes.

Click on one shape then drag the mouse pointer to achieve the required size for the selected shape.

Not only can you rotate, flip and colour shapes, but you can also join them to other standard shapes and objects such as lines and rectangles.

Various shapes have a selection handle that can be used to change such options as size, line endings and arrows.

You can decide to add colour to the body and outline of your AutoShape at any time.

Adding colour to an AutoShape

To add colour to your AutoShape:

1. Select AutoShape.
2. Choose the Fill Color button in the Drawing toolbar.
3. Click the colour of your choice.
4. Confirm.

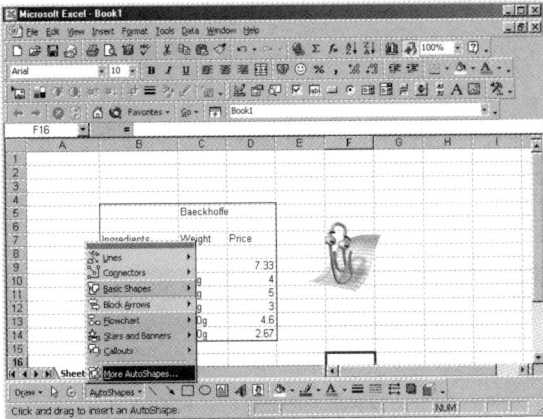

Figure 4.1 AutoShapes pop-up menu.

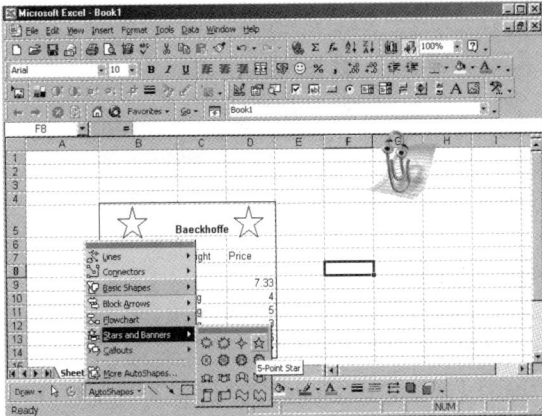

Figure 4.2 Selecting an AutoShape to enhance your work area.

Adding colour to the outline of an AutoShape

To add colour to the outline of your AutoShape:

1. Select AutoShape.
2. Choose the Line Color button in the Drawing toolbar.
3. Click the colour of your choice.
4. Confirm.

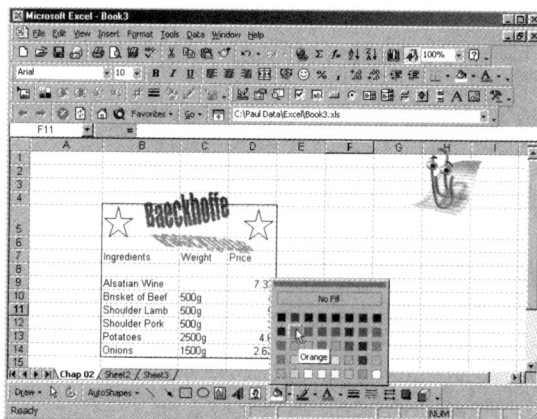

Figure 4.3 Adding colour to your AutoShape and its outline.

Adding text to an AutoShape

Once you have inserted your AutoShape, you can write inside it unless it is a line, connector or freeform.

1. Click the 5-Point Star AutoShape, for example. Your pointer changes to a small cross.
2. Position the little cross on the sheet you want to work with, holding the left mouse button down.
3. Click the text area to write some text inside AutoShape.

Your pointer changes to a four-pointed cross which you drag inside the 5-Point Star AutoShape. Now simply type in the text you wish to insert.

■ Copying graphic objects

You can copy a set of cells from a worksheet or a chart, and paste them as an image in another workbook or another application.

1. Select the cells or the chart.
2. Hold the Shift key down.
3. Open the Edit menu.
4. Click Copy.
5. Select the worksheet or the document where you want to paste the image.
6. Use the Paste command in the application.

■ Importing charts

If you have created a chart in another application, you can copy and paste it in a chart or a worksheet.

To import the whole of a graphic file, in the Insert menu, click Picture, then From File.

You can install various graphic filters which you can use.

If you use Microsoft Office and you have installed Microsoft Clip Gallery, you can insert sound and video clips as well as library pictures.

If you have installed Microsoft Photo Editor, you can scan and import photographs.

■ Inserting a WordArt object

In previous versions of Office, text effects were created with the WordArt program supplied with Office. Since Office 97, you can create these effects directly in your application thanks to a new tool, known as Insert WordArt in the Drawing toolbar, which also has new functions, such as 3D effects and background textures.

With WordArt, you can add 3D effects to lines, to AutoShapes and to freeform objects with the 3D tool in the Drawing toolbar. 3D options allow you to modify the depth of a drawing as well as its colour, its angle, the direction of the light and the reflection on its surface.

1. Open your worksheet.
2. Install your WordArt toolbar.
3. Select your title 'Baeckhoffe'.
4. Delete it by pressing on the Del key.
5. Place-your pointer where you want to insert your new title with special WordArt effects.
6. Click the Insert WordArt button.
7. Select the WordArt effect you prefer.

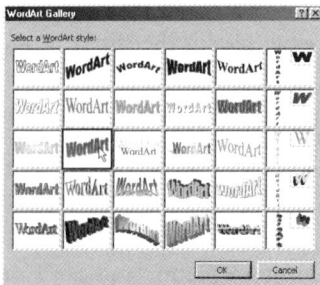

Figure 4.4 Enhance your title with a default WordArt effect.

8. Enter your text in the dialog box adjusting the font size.

9. Confirm.

Your 3D title is now displayed in your work area.

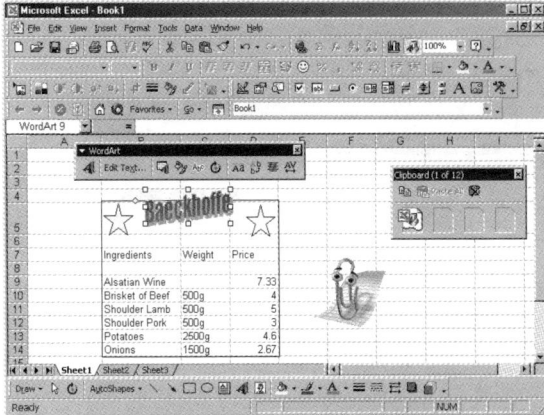

Figure 4.5 A 3D title is displayed in your work area.

Free Rotate

You can apply a free rotation to your title:

1. Select your title.

2. Click the Free Rotate button. The pointer now changes to a black circular arrow which indicates a rotation movement.

3. Decide the rotation angle you require for your title.

4. With the black arrow, position the pointer over a round handle and drag to rotate the title to the required angle.

If the WordArt program is already installed in your computer, it will be kept when you install Office; but you may not be able to use the new Insert WordArt tool to create your text effects. Text effects created in WordArt are not automatically converted into new animated objects.

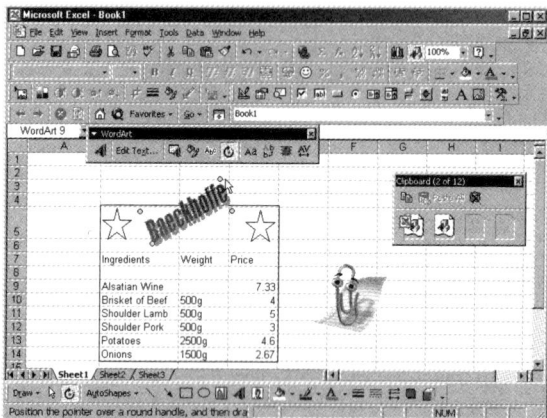

Figure 4.6 The Free Rotate button and the arrow allow you to rotate WordArt objects.

Default rotations

As well as the Free Rotate button, there are four additional default rotation buttons:

- **Left Rotate.** Rotates the selected object by 90° to the left.
- **Right Rotate.** Rotates the selected object by 90° to the right.
- **Horizontal Rotate.** Rotates the selected object by 180° horizontally.
- **Vertical Rotate.** Rotates the selected object by 180° vertically.

These commands are not available if the selected object cannot be rotated, i.e. if it is a picture or an OLE object.

The ABC button

The WordArt Shape option represented by the ABC button allows you to give this title and its new orientation one of the forty available aspects, such as:

- Stop;
- Triangle Up;
- Chevron Up;
- Arch down (Curve);
- Circle (Curve);
- Deflate;
- Wave;
- Inflate...
  for example, choose the Inflate Bottom option.

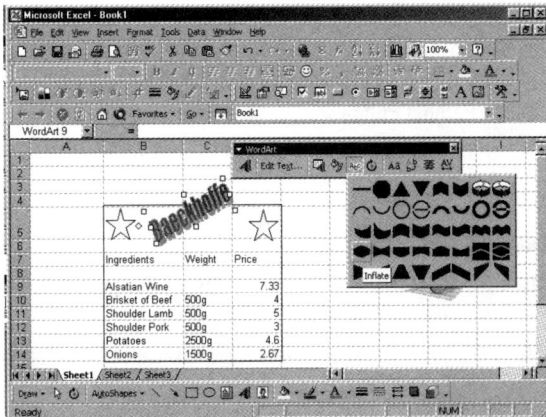

Figure 4.7 Selecting the Inflate Bottom shape in WordArt.

Your title now has the predefined 3D WordArt effect and the
Inflate Bottom effect.

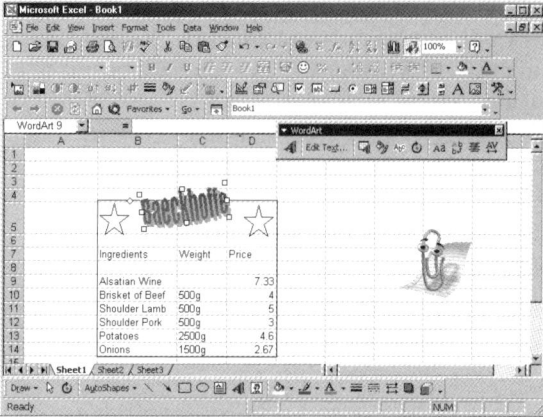

Figure 4.8 Your title and its new layout.

*You cannot display the WordArt object in this mode, and you
cannot check its spelling.*

The Same Letter Heights button

The Same Letter Heights button assigns the same height to all
the letters in the selected WordArt object.

The Vertical Text button

The Vertical Text button puts the letters in the selected
WordArt object one on top of the other, vertically.

■ Using clip art

Clip art is an internal image library of computer drawings
that can be used as illustrations. Clip art, or clips, are often

fairly simple shapes. They are usually quite useful if users do not have any illustrations for their texts and charts. The problem really is that anybody can use these little drawings and therefore they show up on all documents when the author, for one reason or another, has not been able to do enough work in terms of layout. Use with moderation!

Insertion of clip art from other applications

Microsoft Office offers a large variety of charts. You can use them, for instance, as personal logos to add illustrations to your invoices, charts and documents. Finding them is easy:

1. Open the Insert menu.
2. Select the Picture option.
3. Click the ClipArt submenu. This opens the Clip Gallery.
4. Select the most appropriate theme: Plants rather than Buildings.
5. Click the rose.
6. Click the Insert clip command button.

The clip art representing a rose is displayed in the selected position.

■ Adjusting the lighting of a 3D object

Now you wish to produce another title in 3D:

1. Select your title.
2. Click the 3D button in the Drawing toolbar. This button allows you to modify the shape of your title without any intervention on your part.
3. Click the default effect you prefer.
4. Confirm by clicking OK. Your new title in 3D is displayed in your work area.

5. Click this new WordArt object, to select your title in 3D.

6. Click 3D settings at the bottom of the 3D gallery window and then click Lighting in the toolbar.

You can adjust both the intensity and the direction of the light.

1. Start by adjusting the intensity. You have three available options:

   ■ Bright.

   ■ Normal.

   ■ Dim.

2. Click on Bright.

3. Then adjust the direction of the light. You can choose several alternatives:

   ■ From the left.

   ■ From the right.

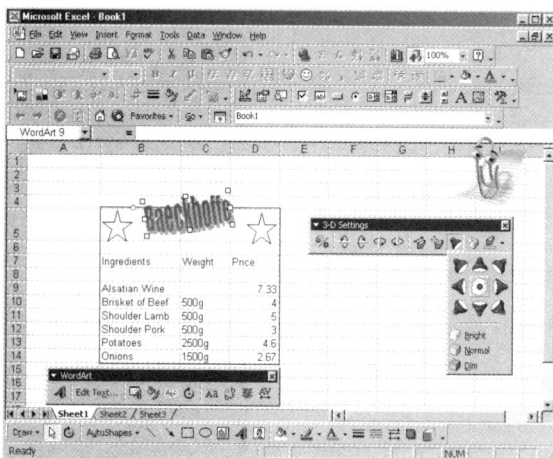

Figure 4.9 Choosing a lighting option.

- From above.
- From below.
- Central...

4. Choose central lighting, for example.

The lighting of your title is immediately adjusted.

■ Modifying a 3D effect

To modify the 3D effect for the title in your sheet, click 3D Settings in the Drawing toolbar, then use the tools in the toolbar 3D Settings.

The ten buttons in the 3D Settings toolbar give you directions for:

- **3D/2D On/Off.** Applies a 3D format to the selected object using the default 3D choices, or cancels the 3D effect. The 3D Layout and 3D Color are mutually exclusive. If you activate the 3D Layout, the 3D Color settings will be deactivated and vice versa.

- **Tilt Down.** The Tilt Down button tilts the 3D effect down by 6° on a horizontal axis. To tilt it up to 45°, hold the Shift key down and click the Tilt Down button.

- **Tilt Up.** The Tilt Up button tilts the 3D effect down by 6° on a horizontal axis. To tilt it up to 45°, hold the Shift key down and click the Tilt Up button.

- **Tilt right.** The Tilt Right button tilts the 3D effect by 6° to the right on a vertical axis. To tilt it up to 45°, hold the Shift key down and click the Tilt Right button.

- **Tilt left.** The Tilt Left button tilts the 3D effect by 6° to the left on a vertical axis. To tilt it up to 45°, hold the Shift key down and click the Tilt Left button.

■ **Depth.** Adjusts the depth of a shape in 3D by 0 points to infinity. A custom option allows you to define the number of points.

■ **Direction.** Adjusts the perspective you wish to give to your object.

■ **Lighting.** Adjusts the brightness for your object from nine different angles.

■ **Surface.** Adjusts the way the surface of your object looks. You have four options: Wire Frame, Matt, Plastic and Metal.

■ **3D Color** (**Automatic**). Defines the colour you want to give your object. It can be Standard or Custom.

Select your title 'Baeckhoffe'. Click Depth in 3D Settings. Adjust the depth, in points, that you wish to assign to your title: 72 points, 144, or infinity, for example.

■ Adding a shadow

You can add a shadow to a shape or to a drawing with the Drawing toolbar by clicking on the Shadow button. You have 26 options, among which are the following:

■ **Move up shadow.** Moves the shadow of the selected objects up incrementally.

■ **Move down shadow.** Moves the shadow of the selected objects down incrementally.

■ **Move shadow to the left.** Moves the shadow of the selected objects to the left incrementally.

■ **Move shadow to the right.** Moves the shadow of the selected objects to the right incrementally.

1. Choose shadow Style 6, for example.
2. Confirm.

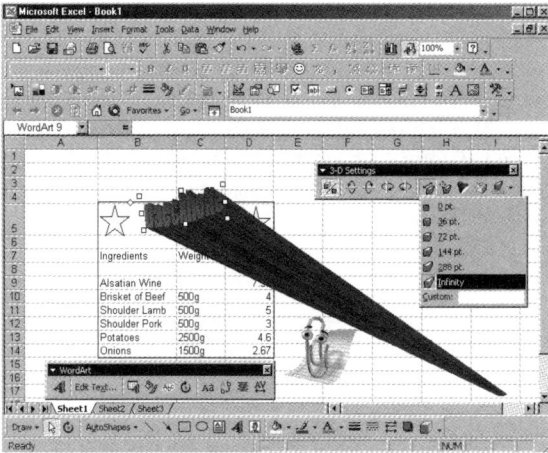

Figure 4.10 Your title with an 'Infinity' depth effect.

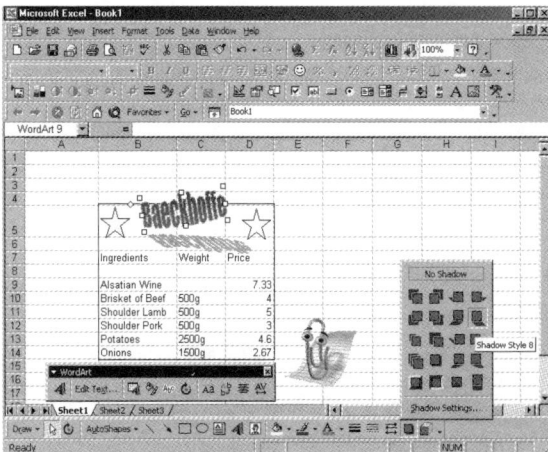

Figure 4.11 Your title is now enhanced by a Style 6 shadow.

Your title and its shadow effects are now displayed on your work area.

Shadow On/Off activates the shadow layout of the selected object by using the default shadow settings, or deactivates it. Shadow and 3D formatting are mutually exclusive. If you activate the shadow format, all 3D settings will be automatically deactivated and vice versa.

5
Executing simple operations

With Microsoft Excel 2000, you can create a large variety of formulas, to carry out simple or more complex operations.

For simple calculations, you can use default formulas. To carry out several operations at the same time and arrive at a single or multiple results, you can use an array formula. If you wish to view the total value for a range of cells, use the automatic subtotals function.

When you select cells, Microsoft Excel 2000 displays the total for the range in the Status bar.

■ Adding

The following operations are executed from the Grafico table (see Grafico.xls).

If your worksheet contains several Subtotals generated with the Sum function, you can arrive at a grand total using the AutoSum function. To arrive at a grand total, click a cell positioned underneath or to the right of the area where the Subtotals are, then click the AutoSum button.

To calculate the total for the articles sold by Grafico, do the following:

1. Click cell B14 where the total will go.
2. Type =. This sign tells Excel that a formula is being created.
3. Select all the cells you wish to include in this formula.

Most important, do not forget to enter the = sign before entering the formula. Otherwise, Excel will not know that you are carrying out an operation.

4. Click cell B9, which contains the number 75. This is the first number to be added. Your cell is surrounded by flashing dotted lines. B9 is also displayed in the Formula bar.

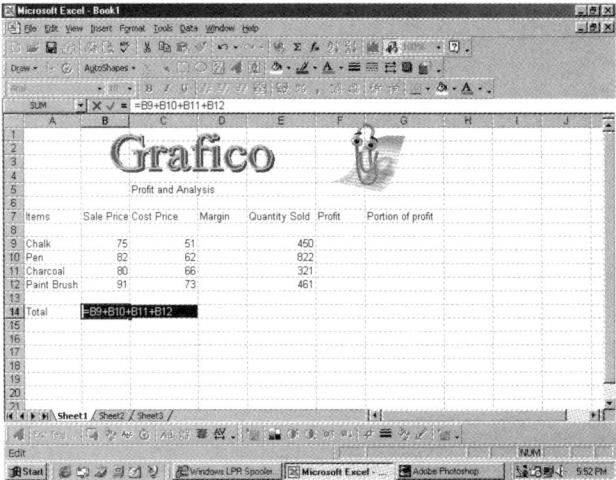

Figure 5.1 Executing an addition operation with Excel 2000.

5. Now type +. This addition sign is known as an 'operator'.

6. Once you have entered the operator, click the next cell, in this case B10, then add +. Repeat this until you get to cell B12.

7. Confirm by pressing the Enter key. Your total is now automatically displayed in the total cell B14.

The AutoSum button

Another way of achieving this is to use the AutoSum button in the Standard toolbar. This is how you do it:

1. Click the cell B14 before doing the total.

2. Click the AutoSum button. The cell range included in the addition is automatically displayed in the Formula bar and in the total cell.

3. Confirm by pressing the Enter key. Your total is automatically displayed in cell B14.

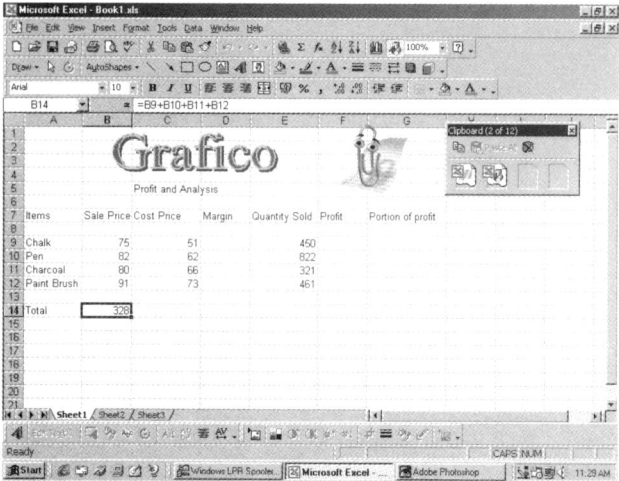

Figure 5.2 The total is automatically displayed in the cell containing the formula.

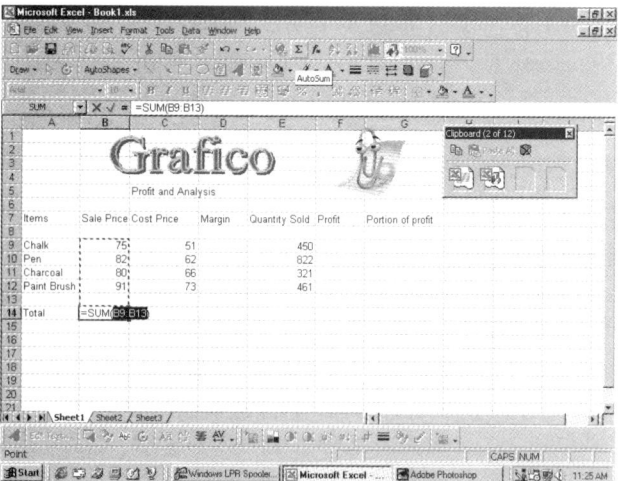

Figure 5.3 Executing an addition operation with the AutoSum button.

In Microsoft Excel, execute an addition operation with the AutoSum function. Excel provides the range of cells to be added. If the proposed range is not the required one, drag the pointer to the range of your choice, then press Enter.

Subtotals

If your worksheet contains several subtotals generated with the Sum function, you can arrive at a grand total of the values using the AutoSum function. To arrive at a grand total, click a cell positioned underneath or to the right of the area which has the subtotals, then click the AutoSum button.

Calculation operators in formulas

Operators indicate the type of calculation to be executed on the elements of the formula.

Excel provides four different types of calculation operators:

- **Arithmetic.** Arithmetic operators execute basic mathematical operations, such as addition, subtraction or multiplication, combine numbers and produce numerical results.

- **Comparison operators.** Comparison operators compare two values and produce the logical value TRUE or FALSE.

- **Text operators.** The & text operator connects or links together two values to produce one continuous text value.

- **Reference operators.** Reference operators combine ranges of cells for calculations with the following operators.

The tables below show the operators for each of these categories.

Arithmetic operators

+	Addition
-	Subtraction/Negative values
*	Multiplication
/	Division
%	Percent
^	Exponential functions

Comparison operators

=	Equal to
>	Greater than
<	Less than
>=	Greater than or equal to
<=	Less than or equal to
<>	Not equal to

Text operator

&	Links together two values to produce one continuous text value.

Reference operators

:	Range operator which produces one reference to all the cells between two references, including the two references.
,	Union operator, which combines multiple references into one reference.

■ Subtracting

Let us assume that you wish the result of the subtraction of B14 and B15 to be displayed in cell B16. To achieve this, do the following:

1. Click in the cell before getting the result of the operation, cell B16 in our example.

2. Enter the = sign then select cell B14. Enter the - sign and click cell B15.

3. Confirm by pressing the Enter key. The result of your subtraction is displayed in cell B16.

■ Multiplying

This time you will multiply cells B14 and B15 and you want the result of the operation to be displayed in cell B16. Follow this procedure:

1. Click the cell before producing the result of the operation (cell B16 in our example).

2. Enter the = sign which tells Excel that you are about to execute an operation.

3. Click the value of cell B14.

4. Enter the x (multiplication) sign in cell B16.

5. Click cell B15.

6. Confirm by pressing the Enter key. The multiplication result is automatically displayed in cell B16.

■■

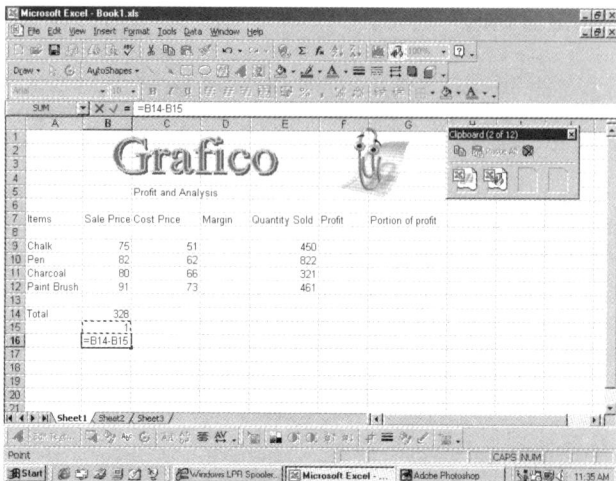

Figure 5.4 Executing a subtraction.

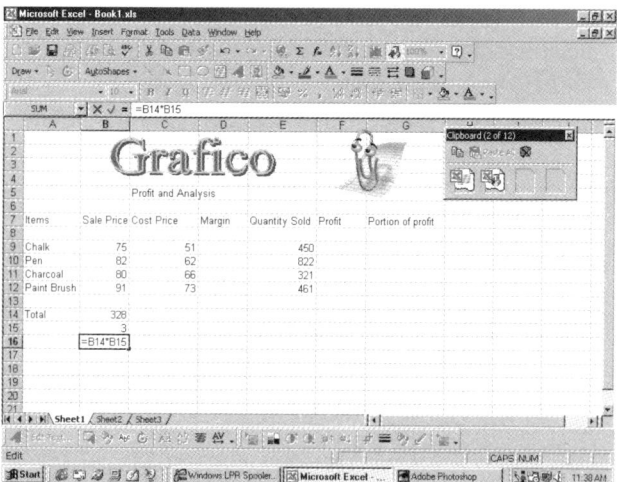

Figure 5.5 Executing a multiplication.

■ Dividing

Let us assume that you wish the result of the division of cell
B14 by cell B15 to be displayed in cell B16. To achieve this,
do the following:

1. Click cell B16, before producing the result of the division
   operation.

2. Enter the = sign in this same cell. This tells Excel that you
   are about to execute an operation.

3. Click cell B14, then enter the division operator / in cell
   B16.

4. Click cell B15 and confirm by pressing the Enter key. The
   division result is automatically displayed.

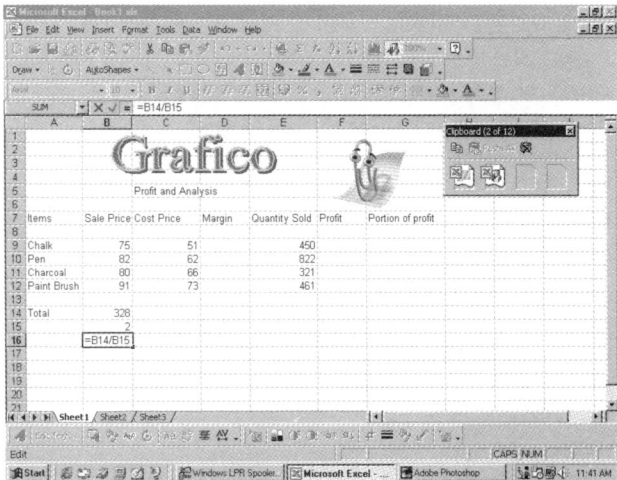

Figure 5.6 Executing a division.

■ Creating a formula

Formulas calculate values by following a specific order, which is their syntax. All Microsoft Excel 2000 formulas start with the = sign followed by the calculation.

In the worksheet of the Grafico company, the 'Realised margin' column is the result of a calculation relating to the 'Sale price' and 'Purchase price' columns.

Margin = Sale price − Purchase price

You are going to generate the formula for the first article, chalks. You will then copy it for the other articles. These are the data you will work with: the sale price for chalks is in cell B9, the purchase price in cell C9 and we want to place the result in cell D9. Follow this procedure:

1. Click D9, the cell which will display the margin for chalks, then type = to tell Excel that this is a calculation formula.

2. Click cell B9, Sale price for chalks. This is automatically displayed with a flashing dashed border and the Formula Bar displays =B9.

3. Type the − sign (the subtraction operator). The dashed border disappears. Excel is waiting for the address of the cell to be subtracted.

4. Click C9, Purchase price for chalks. Confirm by pressing the Enter key. The number 24 is automatically displayed, which is the value of the realised margin, and the Formula bar displays the formula.

■ Copying a formula

When you move a formula, the cells' references in the formula do not change. When you copy a formula, the absolute

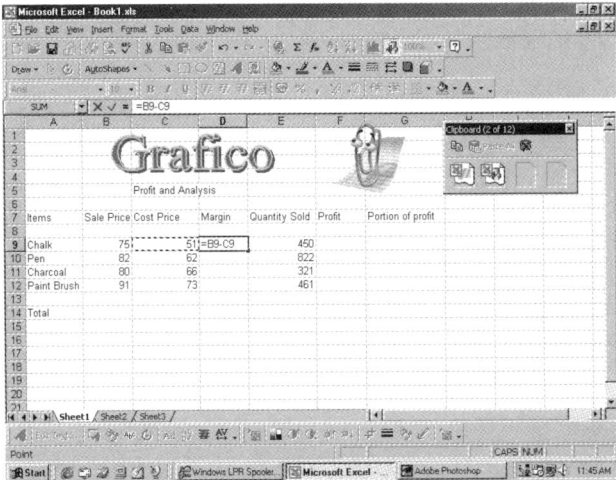

Figure 5.7 Calculating a margin with Excel.

references in cells do not change as opposed to what happens for relative references.

To calculate the margin realised on the sale of other articles, simply copy the formula in cell D9. You can choose the method you prefer from the three methods described here.

First method

1. Select the D9:D12 range.
2. Open the Edit menu.
3. Choose the Copy option and copy it lower down.

You can now view the margins for all articles.

Second method

1. Click cell D9 and position the mouse pointer on the copy fill handle, when the pointer becomes a small black cross, at the bottom right-hand corner of the cell.

2. Hold the left mouse button down while dragging the copy fill handle.

You can now view the margins for all articles.

Third method

1. Go to cell D9. Click the Copy button which shows two pages next to each other. The cell is now surrounded by the flashing dashed border.

2. Select the D10:D12 range.

3. Confirm.

You can now view the margins for all articles.

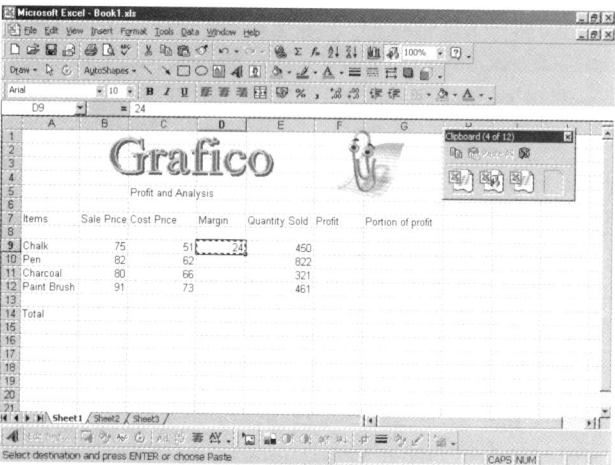

Figure 5.8 Copying a formula with the Copy button.

Relative references

In all three cases, Excel copies the basic formula in cell D9.

When you copy it, the references in the initial formula are automatically adjusted.

What are relative references? This little exercise will show you:

- Go to D10, D11, D12 in turn.
- Check the Formula bar.
- The initial formula B9-C9 is now B10-C10, B11-C11 and B12-C12.

In this way, each formula is always referenced to the two preceding cells on the same row, which means the Sale price and the Purchase price for the corresponding article.

To achieve this result, Excel has simply added to each reference for the initial formula a number of rows corresponding to the position of the copy relating to the original formula.

Absolute references

The cell is an absolute reference when its address does not depend on the position of the formula, but is defined absolutely by its row and column references on your worksheet.

Let us take the example of the calculation of part profits for the Grafico company.

The calculation formula for the realised profit is:

Realised profit for an article = Realised margin for article * Sold quantities

To find the realised profit:

1. Go to cell F9.
2. Select the F9:F12 range.
3. Type formula =D9*E9.

   The realised profit on the sale of chalks is automatically displayed in the cell.
4. Drag the copy fill handle which is in the form of a little black cross.

The realised profit for the articles is automatically displayed in cells F10, F11 and F12.

The calculation formula for Portion of Profit is:

Portion of profit for an article = Realised profit for article/Total profits

1. Position yourself on G9, Portion of Profit, then type =.

2. Click F9, then type /.

3. Click F14, the total realised profit. Once you have obtained the value (in our example, '0,269'), click on the Percent tool. The value is displayed rounded, therefore it becomes 27%. Then copy the formula for the three other articles.

4. Select the G9:G12 range, then copy the formula for the three other articles. You can see that the error value #DIV/0! is automatically displayed in three cells.

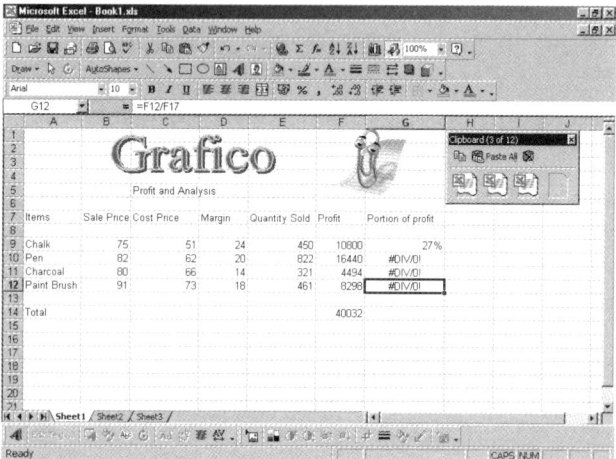

Figure 5.9 The error message is automatically displayed in three cells.

If you go to these three cells, you will see that, in the Formula bar, the initial formula is modified every time. For example, cell G11 tells us that the F11 formula is divided by F16. Or F16 is an empty cell, and the value of an empty cell is zero by default. With its error message, Excel tells you that you are trying to divide by zero.

Instead of entering the three precise formulas for each of the cells, simply modify the initial G9 formula so that the reference to the total realised profit, F14, does not change when it is copied.

Cell F11 must therefore be an **absolute reference** in the G9 formula, which means a cell whose address is not dependent on the position of the formula, but is defined **absolutely** by its row and column references in your worksheet.

■ Calculating an average

Once again, our Grafico worksheet will be used to provide us with an example.

To calculate the average margin, follow these steps:

1. Go to C18.
2. Type =, then Average.
3. Open a bracket.
4. Select the D11:D14 range.
5. Close bracket.
6. Confirm by pressing the Enter key.

Arguments must be numbers, names, arrays or references containing numbers. If an array or a reference entered as the argument contains text, logical values or empty cells, these values are not taken into account. On the other hand, the cells containing the zero value are taken into account.

■■

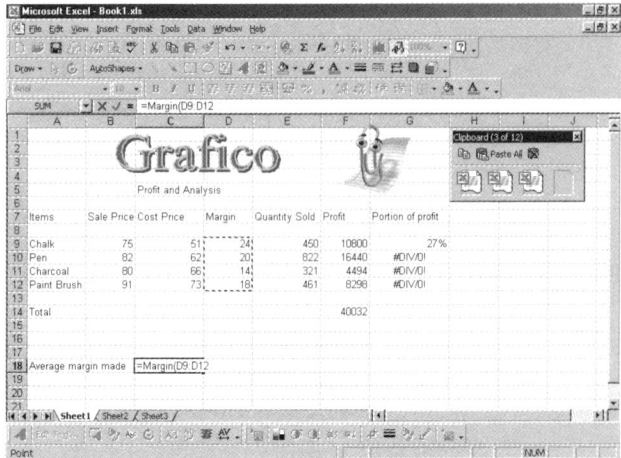

Figure 5.10 Calculating an average.

■ Calculating an average with the Function Wizard

To calculate an average with the Function Wizard, select the Fx icon which is known as 'Paste function'. The Function Wizard is automatically displayed.

To use the Function Wizard, do the following:

1. Double click the AVERAGE option.

2. Now select in the dialog box, in the Number 1 box, the range from which you wish to calculate the average. This is the D11:D14 range.

3. Confirm by pressing the Enter key.

In our example, the result produced is 19.

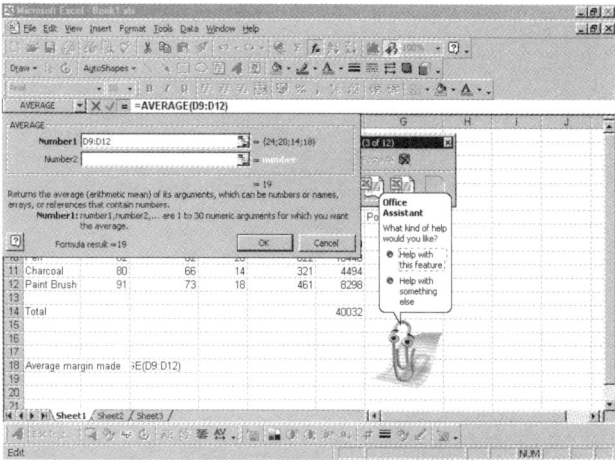

Figure 5.11 Calculating an average with the Function Wizard.

■ Using array formulas

Imagine that you need to fix the sale price for an item which is likely to produce the best profit for you. If the price of your products is too high, you will sell less. If you lower the price, you will sell more. An array calculation in Excel allows you to optimise your profits.

What is an array formula?

The array formula acts on two or more sets of values known as 'array arguments'.

Each array argument must have the same number of rows and columns. You create array formulas in the same way as simple standard formulas, as follows:

1. Select the cells which will contain the formula.
2. Create the formula.
3. Press Ctrl+Shift+Enter to type the formula.

6 Managing cells

■ Collecting cells

With the Clipboard

To collect cells, you can use the Clipboard.

1. Select the range of cells to be collected.
2. Open the Edit menu.
3. Click Cut.
4. Place the active cell on the destination required.
5. Open the Edit menu.
6. Click Paste or Insert and paste.

   ■ The Paste option superimposes the collected cells onto the destination cells.

   ■ Insert and paste inserts the collected cells by moving the old destination cells downwards or to the right.

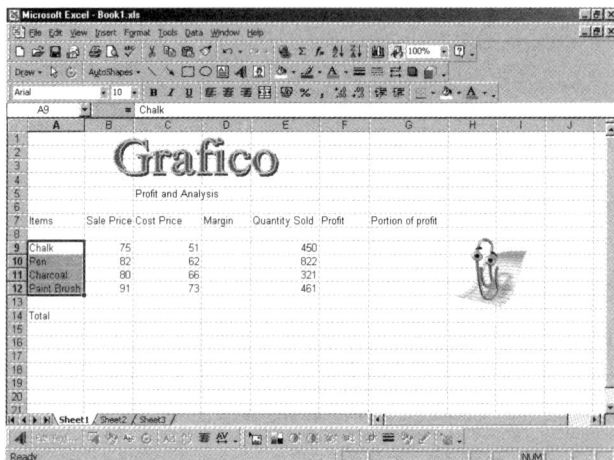

Figure 6.1 The Paste option superimposes the collected cells to the destination cells.

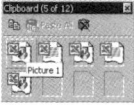

Figure 6.2 The new Clipboard contains up to 12 different objects.

With the mouse

Hold the Ctrl key down while positioning the mouse pointer, which becomes an arrow when it is placed on the edge of the selection area. You can move the selection by clicking and dragging, keeping the Ctrl key pressed.

■ Copying cells

With the Clipboard

Use the same method as for collecting cells.

1. Select the cells to be copied.
2. Open the Edit menu.
3. Click on the Copy option.
4. Point to the destination.
5. Open the Edit menu.
6. Click on Paste or on Insert and paste.

By default, Excel transfers all the attributes present in the source cells. If you only wish to copy specific attributes, open the Edit menu and select the Paste special option, which allows you to select the attributes to be copied. To copy the Clipboard contents to nonadjacent ranges, preselect these ranges.

With the mouse

Hold the Ctrl key down while positioning the mouse pointer, which becomes an arrow, on the edge of the selection area.

Keeping the Ctrl key down, move the selection by clicking and dragging.

■ Incremental copying

An incremental series is a series of words or numbers with a logical sequence.

For example:

- 1, 2, 3, 4, 5
- 3, 6, 9, 12
- Monday, Tuesday, Wednesday

You can automatically fill several types of series selecting the cells and dragging the fill handle or using the Series command.

1. To specify the type of series, define the starting value for the series; for example, 'Monday'.

2. Hold the right mouse button down and drag the fill handle.

Defining a customised list

A text can be incremented if the list is defined by the user, or if you are dealing with names of months or days of the week. To access the customised list:

- Open the Tools menu.
- Select Options.
- Click the Custom Lists tab.
- Choose the new series that you wish to increment.

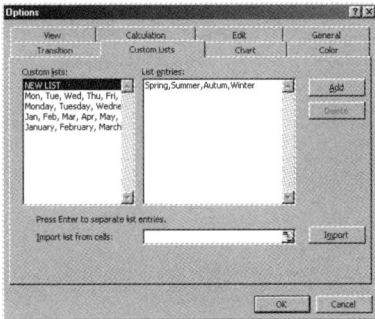

Figure 6.3 Create your incremental series from the Options dialog box.

■ Protecting cells

Modifying the contents of cells, which include constants or formulas.

Recreating a constant is easy. Recreating a complex formula is a little more complicated, therefore you should protect your data. Excel comes with a security system, Protect Sheets, which allows you to stop unwanted modifications.

To start with, all cells have a Locked status.

To access this:

- Open the Format menu.
- Select Cells.
- Click the Protection tab.

The Format cell dialog box warns you that locking cells or hiding formulas has no effect unless the worksheet is protected.

■■■■■■■■■■■■■■■■■■■■■■■■ ■ ■ ■ ■ ■ ■ ■ ■ ■ ■ ■ ■ ■

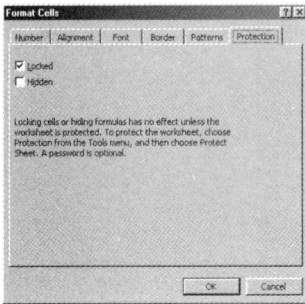

Figure 6.4 Tick the 'Locked' check box to lock the cell.

To protect your worksheet, this is what you must do:

1. Open the Tools menu.
2. Select the Protection submenu.
3. Choose Protect Sheet.

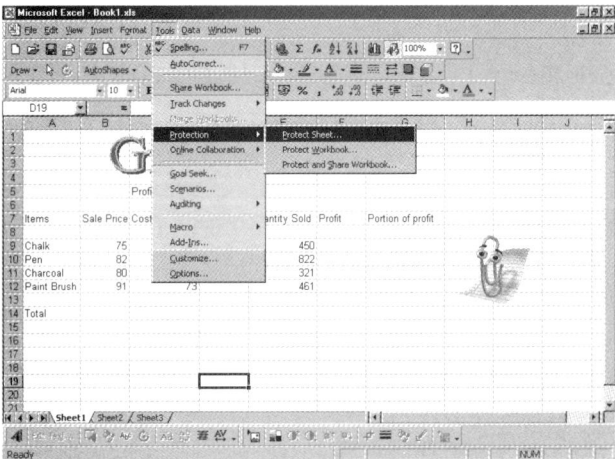

Figure 6.5 The Protect Sheet option in the Tools menu.

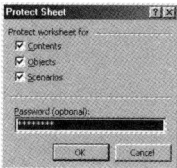

Figure 6.6 Choose your password.

A dialog box is displayed. Enter a password, for example 'Oxymoron'.

To confirm your password, reenter it in the second dialog box, with exactly the same spelling.

If you lose or forget your password, you will have no way of recovering it. It is therefore advisable to keep a list of passwords and their corresponding workbook and sheet names in a safe place; when typing the password, remember that passwords are case-sensitive.

All the cells in your worksheet are now write-protected.

If you attempt to modify the contents of one of these cells, Excel displays the following warning:

'The cell or chart you are trying to change is protected and therefore read-only.'

The warning message then explains how to remove protection.

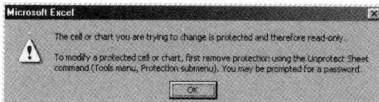

Figure 6.7 Warning against modifying a locked cell.

Unprotect

This is how you remove protection:

1. Open the Tools menu.
2. Select the Protection option.
3. Click Unprotect Sheet.

A dialog box called Unprotect Sheet is automatically displayed; enter your password.

You can now rewrite in all the cells in your worksheet.

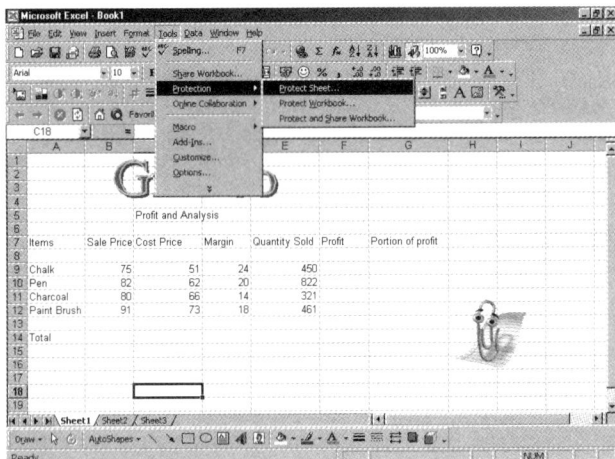

Figure 6.8 The Unprotect option.

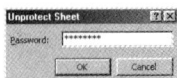

Figure 6.9 The Unprotect Sheet dialog box.

■ Naming a cell range

The usual row–column references are not the best to use in formulas, especially when cells are fairly long.

Excel allows you to assign a name, given by the user, to a cell or a cell range. These names may be used instead of the references in all current operations.

Assigning a name

To name a cell range:

1. Select the D7:D12 cells range with the column header 'Margin'.
2. Open the Insert menu.
3. Select the Name, Define submenu.
4. Click Define.

The Name in the workbook is Margin and corresponds to the D7:D12 cell range.

Rather than using the D7:D12 values to designate the area, you can simply define it with the name: Margin.

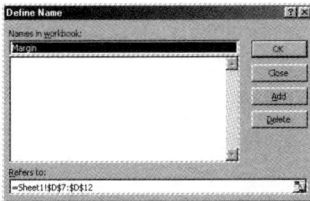

Figure 6.10 Type the name 'Margin' in the text area in the Define Name dialog box.

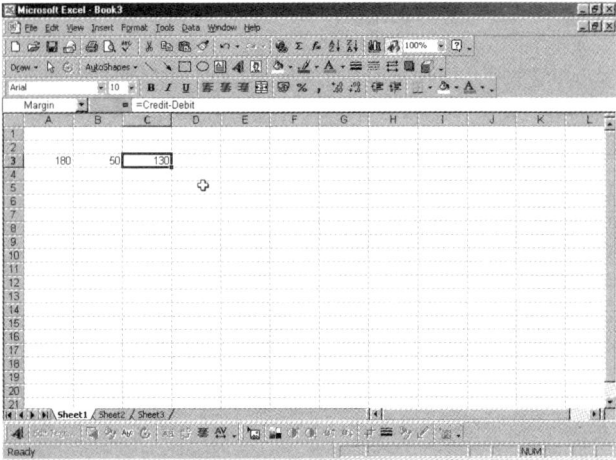

Figure 6.11 Executing an operation using names.

Using names

A cell name can replace the reference for that cell in all calculation or reference operations. Simply type the name of the cell or of the range instead of its address.

To use a name:

1. Click on the drop-down list positioned to the right of the active cell.
2. Select in the list the name you want.
3. Use the Insert, Name, Paste command.

Example 1:

1. A3 contains 180 and has the name Credit.
2. B3 contains 50 and has the name Debit.
3. C3 will contain the result and has the name Sale.
4. Go to C3.

5. Instead of entering the formula = A2-B2, enter = Credit-Debit.

Assigning a name to a formula

When you define a name, in the Refer to box, you can enter a full expression. This allows you to use the name instead of the formula. In all formulas, VAT will automatically be replaced by 17.5 %. The formula will therefore become: =L(5)C*17.5 %, and not =L(5)C*VAT.

Figure 6.12 The Refer to box.

■ Displaying data

Let us assume that you wish to find the D7:D12 cells range you have called Margin:

1. Open the Edit menu.
2. Click the Go To option. A dialog box is displayed, which shows the name previously assigned to the D7:D12 range, Margin.
3. Confirm. Margin is automatically displayed as selected in your work area.

Figure 6.13 The Go To function.

The Find, Replace and Go To are extremely useful when searching long documents.

■ Searching for data

To update data, text or numbers, in a worksheet, this is what you do:

1. Open the Edit menu.
2. Select the Find option.
3. Type now in the dialog box the text or the number you wish to find; let us say, for example, that this is the word 'Margin', positioned in cell A13, at the intersection of row 13 and column A.
4. Click Find Next.

Your selection area now shows the word 'Margin' which you were looking for.

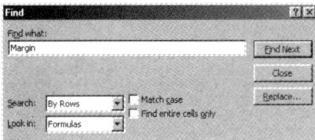

Figure 6.14 The Find function in the Edit menu.

■ Replacing data

Let us imagine that you wish to replace the word 'Charcoal' with 'Pencils' in your work area for the Grafico company:

1. Open the Edit menu.
2. Select the Find option.

3. Fill the dialog box by typing Charcoal in the Find what box.

4. Click the Replace command button.

5. Type Pencils in the Replace box.

6. Click Find Next.

Excel finds the word 'Charcoal' and replaces it with the new word. 'Pencils' is automatically displayed in the worksheet for the Grafico company.

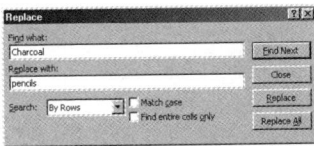

Figure 6.15 The Find and Replace functions in the Edit menu.

■ Correcting data

To correct data, this is what you do:

1. Open the Tools menu.

2. Use the Spelling command.

3. You can also click on the button for this command displayed as ABC.

The Spelling button is is marked with the letters ABC with a tick underneath. Excel can check the spelling of the active document, file or workbook.

The spell checker then corrects the spelling for the Grafico sheet. No error is flagged in the text, but the word Margin is reported to be Not in Dictionary. You can ignore this comment or you can add the word to the dictionary. You may decide to increase your dictionary by clicking on the Add option.

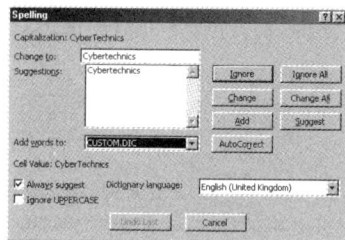

Figure 6.16 The spell checker checks the spelling for the contents of cells.

Misspell the word 'Scissors' on purpose replacing the 'c' with 's'. Put your worksheet through the spell checker.

The AutoCorrect command automatically corrects the most usual typing errors. Your word 'Ssissors' is immediately flagged as not in dictionary. In the dialog box, delete it and write it correctly. Click now on the Change button. Your word is automatically displayed as correctly spelt in your worksheet.

■ Sorting and filtering data

To sort data:

1. Select the range to be sorted.
2. Click the Data menu.
3. Click the Sort option.
4. Choose one, two or three sorting methods in order of importance.
5. Use the drag and drop technique.

The ascending order included the following hierarchy:

■ numbers;
■ text;

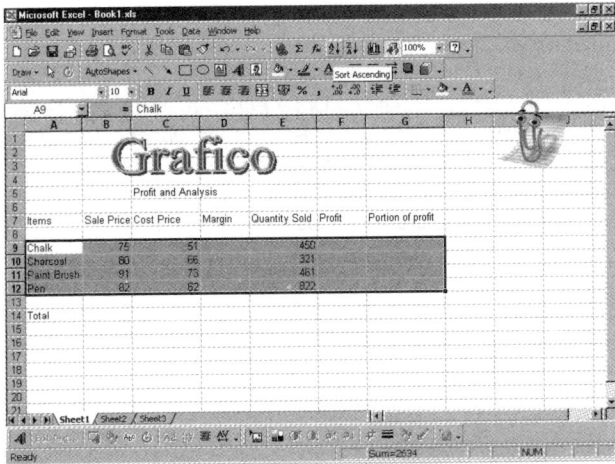

Figure 6.17 Sort your data by alphabetical order.

- logical values;
- empty cells.

If you wish to sort data by alphabetical order, you must select the area to which you wish the sorting to be applied. If you want to sort the articles by alphabetical order:

1. Select the A9:F12 range, which includes the articles, without the title row.
2. Open the Data menu.
3. Click the Sort option.
4. You can click directly on the AZ Sort by Ascending Order button.

    The dialog box which is automatically displayed prompts you to confirm Sort by Ascending Order for column A.
5. Confirm by clicking OK.

The articles in your sheet are displayed as sorted by alphabetical order.

Click the Sort by Ascending Order button to sort your selected elements starting with the first letter of the alphabet, the smallest number or the oldest date. Sorting is carried out on the column containing the insertion point. If you have defined other sorting options beforehand, these will still apply.

7
Exploring advanced functions

■ ■

Creating an outline
Using an outline
Implementing a consolidation
Consolidating data by category
Consolidating data by position
Modifying a consolidation
Creating a PivotTable

■ Creating an outline

An outline allows you to introduce a hierarchy to rows or columns. It is the same procedure as for dividing a book into chapters and paragraphs. In the worksheet, you can display the global results without the details, just like in the table of contents in a book. An outline can be created automatically or manually.

You have four commands:

- **Show details.** Creates and displays the outline symbols on the worksheet. If the symbols are already displayed in an existing outline, clicking on Show details will hide them.

- **PivotTable and PivotChart Report.** Opens the PivotTable and PivotChart Wizard which will guide you in the creation or modification of a PivotTable.

- **Ungroup.** Deletes selected rows or columns within a group in a worksheet in outline mode. In an interactive sheet, this command ungroups each group occurrence and resets the group's original individual elements. For example, quarters are divided into original individual dates.

- **Group.** Defines the selected rows or columns with detailed data within the group which is part of an outline, for summary purposes. If the outline was not created, this command will create it. In a PivotTable, this command groups elements by category to create a single element from several elements. You can group, for example, days, weeks, months or other dates as a quarter to carry out your analysis, produce a chart or go to print.

Excel 2000 uses calculation formulas to arrive at the outline hierarchy.

If the worksheet is properly structured, this method works very well.

Auto Outline

1. Select the sheet for which you wish to create an outline.

2. Open the Data menu.

3. Select the Group option and create an outline.

4. Click the Auto Outline button.

You will immediately see that there are two outline levels in our example.

For vertical outline:

- sales by town;
- sales by country.

For horizontal outline:

- sales by month;
- sales by quarter.

Your outline allows you to create a table of summary data for the worksheet.

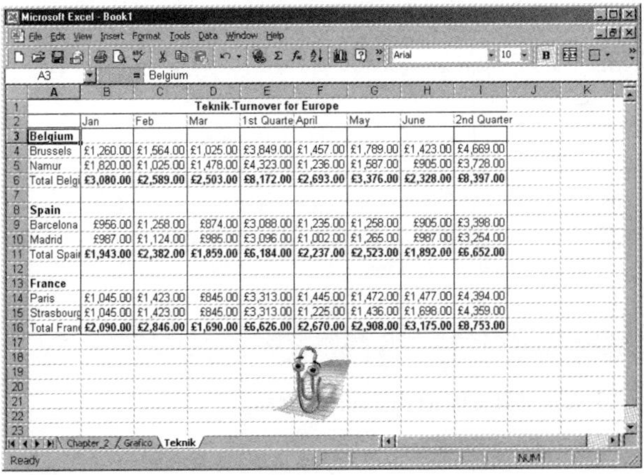

Figure 7.1 Your worksheet structure.

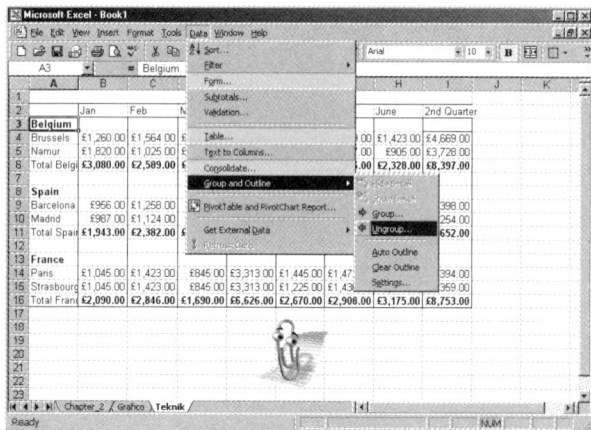

Figure 7.2 The outline mode is accessible from the Data menu.

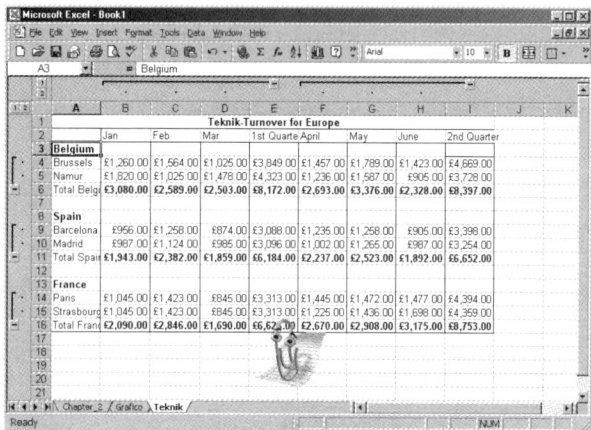

Figure 7.3 Your outline is created automatically.

- To increase or decrease the outline level, click the Plus and Minus buttons.
- To display the outline levels, click the 1 and 2 buttons.

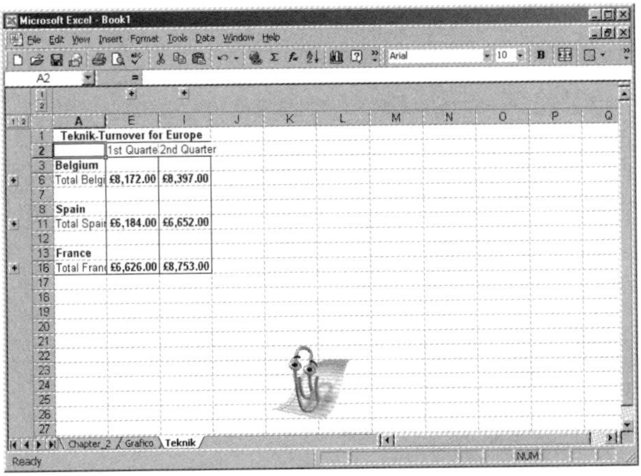

Figure 7.4 Your work area draws all the information together.

Manual creation of an outline

Select the topmost hierarchical position to finish with the lowest one, descending the previous hierarchy level by level by clicking the Group button each time.

■ Using an outline

The Show Detail button automatically displays:

- the level bars;
- the decrease (+) and decrease (–) buttons;
- the level buttons for row 1 and 2.

Visible or invisible cells

When an outline is decreased and only shows the main hierarchies (in our example, totals by country and by quarter),
and you copy the selected area, invisible cells are also copied
or represented.

To remedy this:

1. Select the cells range after hiding the lower hierarchies.
2. Click the Select visible cells button.

Style modification

There are several default styles for different outline develop-
ments.

To choose new styles:

1. Open the Data menu.
2. Point to Group and Outline.
3. Click Settings.
4. Select Automatic styles.
5. Click the Create command button.

You can modify these styles exactly like the other data. Do
the following:

1. Open the Format menu.
2. Select the Style command.
3. Click the Modify command button.

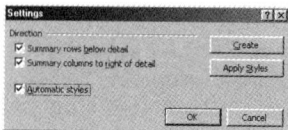

Figure 7.5 The Settings dialog box and its Create option.

■ Implementing a consolidation

With Excel 2000, you can consolidate several worksheets.

You will now consolidate data; for example, the profit from the sale of graphic material for the two shops which are part of the Grafico company.

1. Create two tables which look the same.

2. Choose the data. The quantities sold and the profits realised are different for the two shops.

3. Name your two new worksheets Shop 1 and Shop 2.

   In the example, we are showing them in the same worksheet, but you must keep them on separate worksheets.

4. Open a new worksheet.

5. Rename this worksheet Synthesis.

6. Copy the non-variable elements from the table, in this case the articles, sale price, purchase price.

7. Leave the quantity Sold column empty.

8. Open the Data menu.

9. Click on the Consolidate option. In the Function dropdown list, there are several consolidation options. Select one which is most used in your tables, Shop 1 and Shop 2; in this case, this is Sum, because you wish to consolidate the profits for two shops. But you could also add Maximum, Minimum, Product. The source worksheets for Shops 1 and 2, named Grafico1 and Grafico2, do not need to be open.

10. Select the destination area in the worksheet named Synthesis which will receive the consolidation. This range is F4:F7, which displays the consolidated profit for Shops 1 and 2.

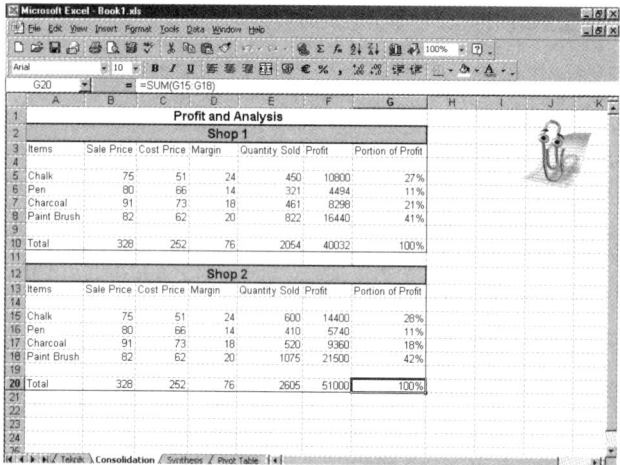

Figure 7.6 Profits made by Shops 1 and 2.

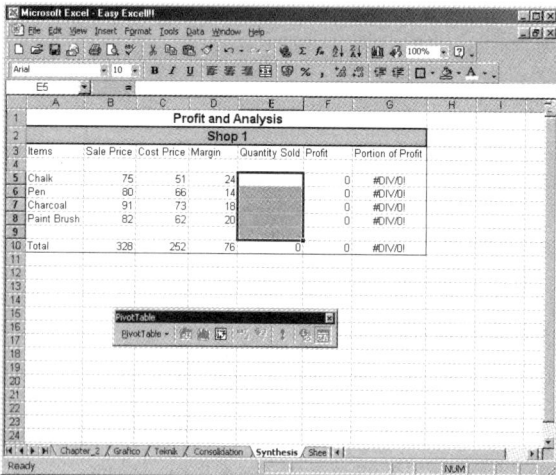

Figure 7.7 The profit consolidation worksheet.

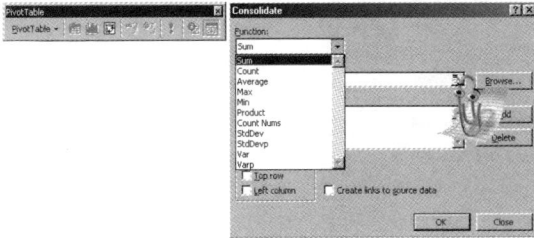

Figure 7.8 The Consolidate dialog box.

11. Open the Data menu.

12. Select the Consolidate option.

13. Choose the type of consolidation (Sum, Product, Average, and so on.).

14. Click in the Reference box and type the source range for Shop 1 or select it yourself in one of the worksheets in the workbook.

15. Click in the Add box.

16. Repeat the operation for all the the sources ranges (in this example, you only have two).

17. Click OK to implement the consolidation.

Consolidation calculations are immediately displayed in your Consolidated profits worksheet.

i

If you tick the Create links to source data box, you can import all the detailed data from the source range, but a generated outline will hide them. If there are no links, Excel only consolidates final values.

Excel 2000

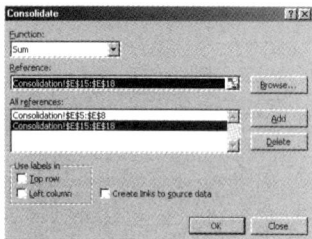

Figure 7.9 Source references in the Consolidate dialog box.

Figure 7.10 Consolidation calculations are displayed in your Consolidated profits table.

■ Consolidating data by category

This method is useful when data to be consolidated are not in the same cell range on their respective worksheet (which was not the case in the chosen example), but share a common title.

It is easy to include in the source area and destination the titles which allow Excel to find again the areas in question at consolidation time.

■ Consolidating data by position

This method is useful when data to be consolidated are all in the same position in the set of source worksheets (which was the case in the chosen example). It is not necessary to include the titles in the area definitions.

■ Modifying a consolidation

Simply select another consolidation type (Average, Min, Max, and so on) in the drop-down list of functions to consolidate, and Excel will proceed immediately to new operations in the consolidation area.

To delete a source area:

1. Select the area to be deleted.
2. Click the Delete button.

To add a source area:

1. Select the Browse box.
2. Enter the new references.
3. Click the Add button.

■ Creating a PivotTable

What is a PivotTable?

The PivotTable is a tool which allows you view the same table in different forms, in a simple, quick and efficient way. If you are using a large complex table, it is totally feasible that different end users will require different types of information.

For example, let us imagine a class with five pupils where three subjects are taught: French, Maths, English.

Depending on whether the sheet is meant for the pupils, their parents or their teachers, the approach will be different. The table will need to highlight different type of information. This diversity of approach is what makes the worksheet truly interactive.

- Parents like to be able to read clear reports on their children, and make comparisons with other pupils.

- Teachers are particularly interested in their subject.

- Pupils are usually only interested in their own results.

The larger the table, the more time is saved by using PivotTable Wizard. With the Wizard, without modifying the data, you will be able to produce different presentations tailor-made for each end user. Better still, you will be able to treat each presentation according to its end use. In practice, the created interactive sheet offers synthetic results which can be reworked and sorted whenever you want, before transforming them into charts.

For example, you will be able to sort pupils:

- by alphabetical order;

- by result in order of excellence;

- by average marks in English;

- by average marks in French;

- by average marks in Maths.

Interactive PivotTable allows a document to be displayed according to the expected information. Data are entered once and reproduced several times in different ways.

The interactive PivotTable toolbar

The interactive PivotTable toolbar has the following functions:

- **Ungroup.** In an interactive PivotTable, this command ungroups each grouped element and re-establishes the individual original elements of the group. Example: terms are divided into original dates.

- **Group.** In an interactive PivotTable, this command groups elements by category to create a unique element from several elements. Example: days, weeks and months can be grouped as terms.

- **PivotTable Wizard.** It takes you through all the steps for creating and implementing an interactive PivotTable.

- **Calculated field.** In an interactive PivotTable, it is a field on which you can operate directly or indirectly.

- **Select Label.** In an interactive PivotTable, this command only selects the labels when you click one label for the interactive field, and not the associated data.

- **Select Data.** In an interactive PivotTable, this command selects only data when you click the interactive data field, and not the associated label.

- **Select Label and Data.** In an interactive PivotTable, this command selects only data and labels when you click the label for the interactive field.

Before using PivotTable Wizard, you must first create your work area and enter your data. Let us get back to our example of a class of five pupils and three taught subjects, for the months of January, February and March.

1. Assign a mark out of 20 to each child.

2. Prepare your work area carefully.

3. Select your work area. The data range you wish to use for your PivotTable must include the set of columns and rows headings.

4. Click Wizard to create an interactive PivotTable.

The first step for creating your PivotTable is to define the starting point for the data, as well as the shape of the presentation.

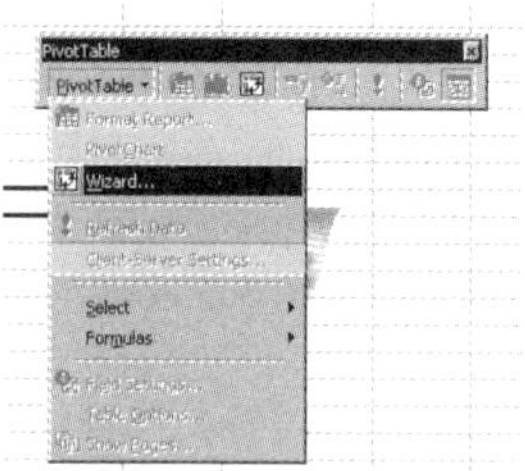

Figure 7.11 The PivotTable toolbar.

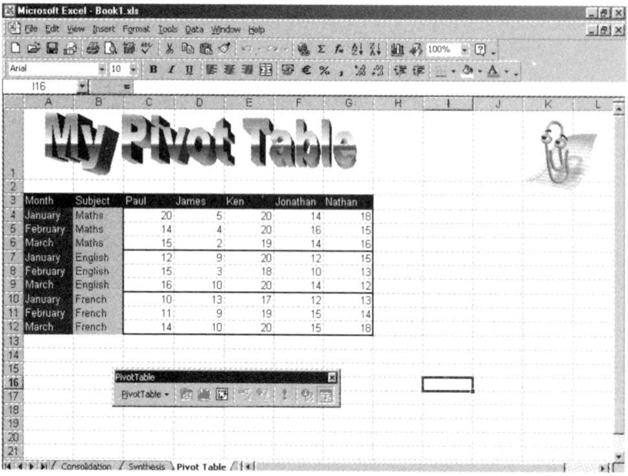

Figure 7.12 In the starting sheet, on the left, the month and subject records will be the future pivots.

The second step allows you to reach the area which defines the table. Since we have been careful to carry out this operation before launching the Wizard, the data will automatically go to the corresponding area.

The third step is the most important. It defines the structure of the table and its options. For example, you may decide

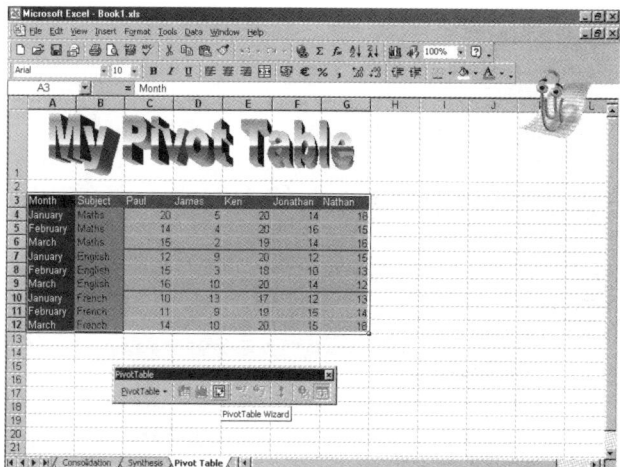

Figure 7.13 The table is selected, and the Wizard is launched.

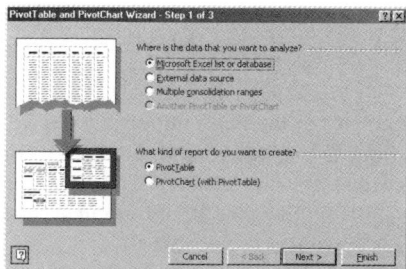

Figure 7.14 Step 1. The data are on the Excel worksheet, but they could also come from an external data source.

that the resulting sheet will be put in a new worksheet, or in the same worksheet.

You must now click the two buttons in the bottom row, on the left.

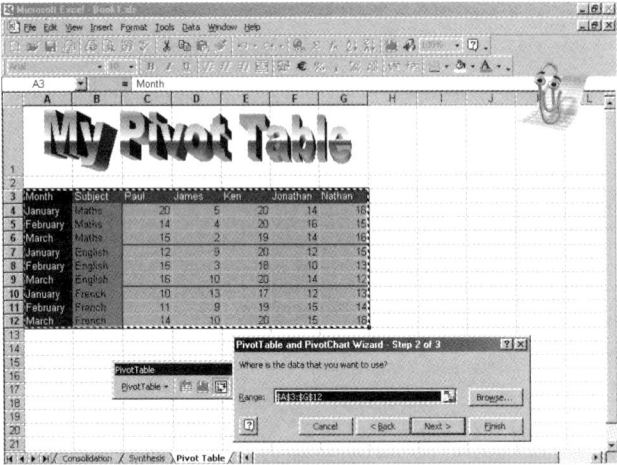

Figure 7.15 Step 2. Selecting the data area.

Let us start by clicking the Options button, which displays various available choices. Deselect them all, before clicking OK.

Click the Layout button. This is the most important step for your work. This conditions the structure and the ease of use of the interactive PivotTable. Be careful, there is no security at this level, and Excel 2000 will have no hesitation in accepting an absurd task if this is what you ask for.

To make your work simpler, we will do it the wrong way round, starting from the right towards the left. In practice, the Page box is only useful for more complex tables than this one. Starting with this would therefore be a mistake.

In the third step you are prompted to construct your PivotTable by dragging the field buttons on the record.

Your PivotTable is now created. It is up to you now to interpret it according to the approach you are interested in.

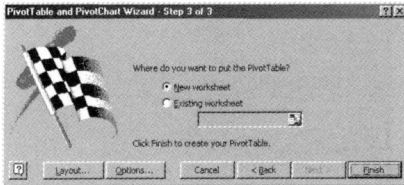

Figure 7.16 Step 3. Displaying the results in a new worksheet.

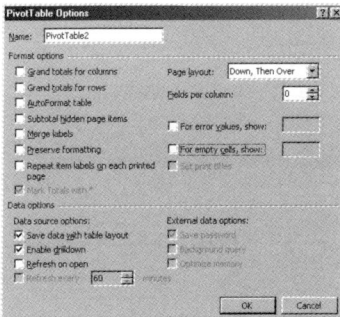

Figure 7.17 After clicking on the Options button, deselect all the choices.

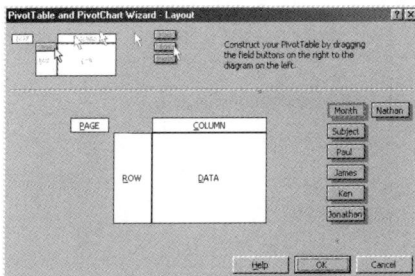

Figure 7.18 The most important step for creating tables consists in setting the records.

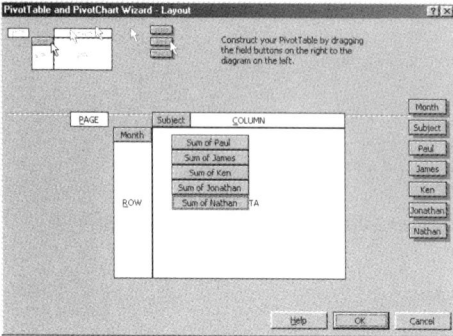

Figure 7.19 This choice guarantees that the display is totally clear.

By opening the subject list, you can obtain the separate averages for each course.

By opening the month list, you can obtain a detailed or summary list for each month.

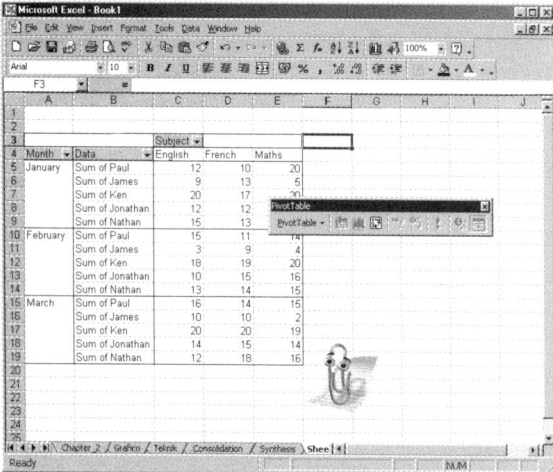

Figure 7.20 Your PivotTable is complete.

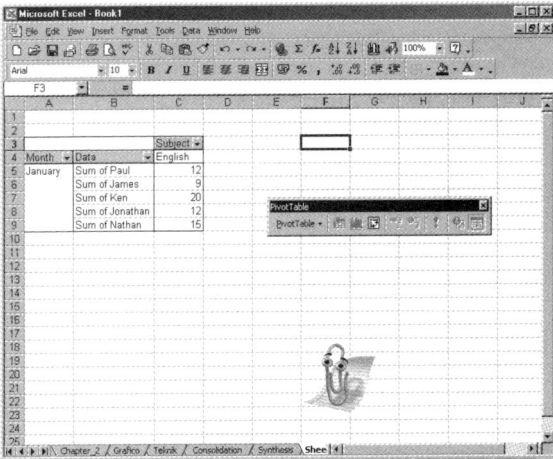

Figure 7.21 You can view the results for one pupil for one subject, for example.

By joining the two, you can customise your request.

Caution, a little bug in early versions does not allow you to select data of the Sum type (in this case a pupil) and only one argument, and then go back to the previous position.

But there are many other things you can do, apart from various displays, as you will see with the other work that we will be doing here. Create two Average records, as shown in Figure 7.22.

A PivotTable can be compared to consecutively parked worksheets, which will then be represented by a single worksheet. The underlying principle is the superimposition of columns, for representing the additional dimension. Starting from a complete, but somewhat jumbled, document, the PivotTable will produce a clearer presentation. The Page diagram allows you to reproduce the original layering of information. For example, if the Page diagram corresponds to the months, by clicking on a drop-down list, you will get all the results for a given month. If the page represents Subject, the drop-down list will propose a summary table for the results for the chosen subject. If the Page diagram is not filled, the sheet will be more complete, but also more difficult to read.

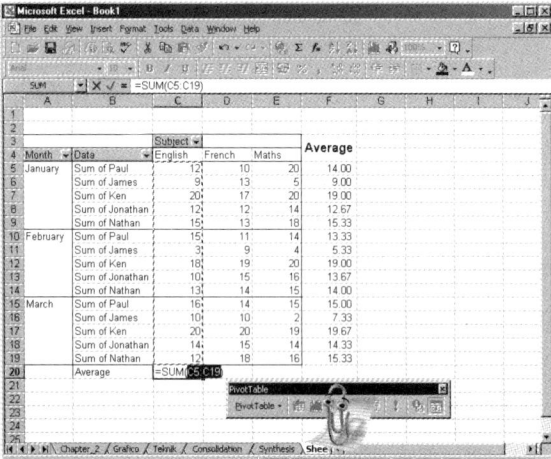

Figure 7.22 Creating two average columns will give much added value to your manipulations of the interactive PivotTable.

The average rows are created around the table when this is displayed at its maximum size. Now the averages are displayed according to the status of your table. For example, Figure 7.23 only displays the averages for the selected months.

Error messages for division by zero are not significant, since no values are taken into account. For advanced programming, it is possible not to display them. Please make reference to other Pearson publications for more advanced users.

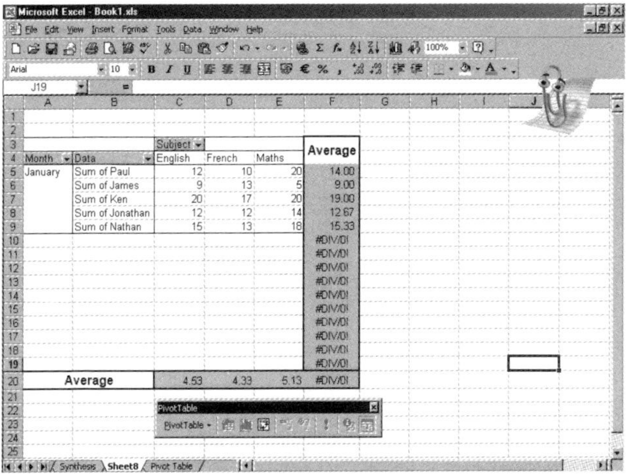

Figure 7.23 Single displayed values are taken into account for additional calculations.

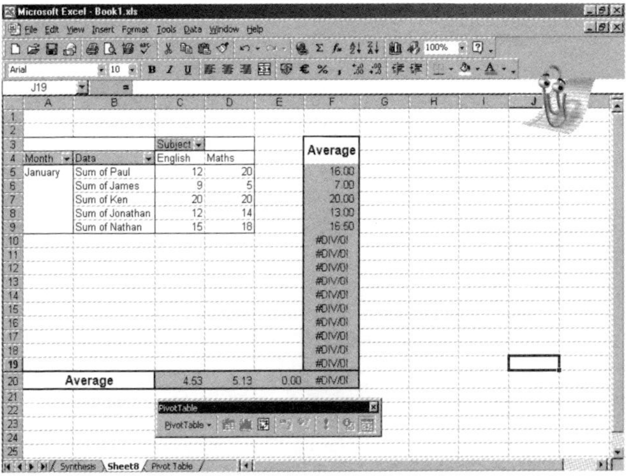

Figure 7.24 Another example of a customised display.

8 Creating a database

■ Databases

What is a database?

A database is a tool which allows you to manage, extract and filter information, then calculate and analyse data.

A database always starts with a first row which describes the file structure. Data must start immediately after the box name. Box names cannot contain punctuation signs or spaces.

It should not contain words which have the same spelling.

Creating a database

The Grafico company has various data on their clients. The person in charge of customer care wants to know the name of each client, their telephone number and the amount of their last order.

These three headers, Name, Telephone and Latest Order are the structure, which means they are the database FIELDS.

You are going to create this database, this list of information, directly in your worksheet.

The first operation consists in keying in the names for the headers on a single row.

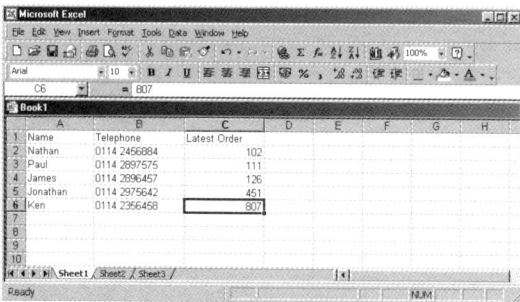

Figure 8.1 Choose the name for the headers.

Enter data exactly one row under the headers.

Each box contains data of the same nature.

■ Using the Entry form

This command displays a form in a dialog box. You can use the data form to view, modify, add, delete and find entries contained in a list or a database.

The Entry form allows you to handle files in a database.

You can create your database using the Entry form:

1. Open the Data menu.
2. Click the Form option.

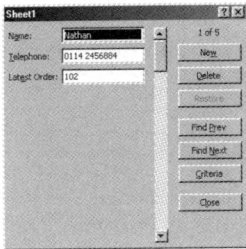

Figure 8.2 The Entry form dialog box.

Entering a file

To enter a file:

1. Place the pointer on the next row in your database.
2. Click New.
3. Choose the data.
4. Click New to confirm the current file.

This is automatically displayed after the others.

Excel automatically enters all the database fields in the Entry box. The software also offers various commands which allow you to move within the database, to add and delete files, and to use specific selection conditions.

Custom formats

Excel has some default formats to which you can add custom formats created by you.

Custom formats are useful for defining the thousands separators, the number of decimal places, the currency symbol or the unit of measure.

To access this Format Cells dialog box:

1. Open the Format menu.

2. Select the Cells option.

3. Click the Number tab.

In the drop-down Category list, you will find the following categories for numbers:

- **General.** General format cells have no specific number format. This is the default number format.

- **Number.** This category is used for general display of numbers. If you click this, you will see a dialog box with a box which allows you to specify the number of digits displayed to the right of the decimal point, a 1000 Separator check box, and another box which allows you to specify how negative numbers are displayed.

- **Currency.** Currency formats are used for general monetary values. The drop-down list Symbol displays all the international currency symbols.

- **Accounting.** Accounting formats line up the currency symbols and decimal points in a column.

- **Date.** Date formats display date and time serial numbers as date values. Use Time formats to display just the time portion.

- **Time.** Time formats display date and time serial numbers as time values. Use Date formats to display just the date portion.

- **Percentage.** Percentage formats multiply the cell value by 100 and displays the result with a percent symbol.

- **Fraction.** Fraction formats propose fractions up to three digits.

- **Scientific.** Allows you to specify the number of digits displayed to the right of the decimal point.

- **Text.** Text format cells are treated as text even when a number is in the cell. The cell is displayed exactly as entered.

- **Special.** Special formats are useful for tackling list and database values.

- **Custom.** Type the number format code, using one of the existing codes as a starting point.

A practical application of these various custom formats would be, for example, the way you display telephone numbers in your database.

To enter a telephone number:

1. Enter your telephone number, digit after digit, including the area code, without worrying about the format.
2. Select it.
3. Open the Format menu.
4. Click Cells.
5. Click the Number tab.
6. Choose Special.
7. Click Phone number in the Type drop-down list.
8. Confirm by clicking OK.

Your telephone number is automatically displayed in the database with the area code in brackets.

Adding a file

To add a file:

1. Click on New.
2. Open the Data menu.
3. Select the Form option.
4. Select the command New.
5. Choose your new file.

Deleting a file

To delete a file:

1. Click anywhere in your database to activate it.
2. Open the Data menu.
3. Select the Form option.
4. Select the file you wish to delete.
5. Click the Delete button. A message is automatically displayed on your screen warning you that the file will be permanently deleted.
6. Confirm.

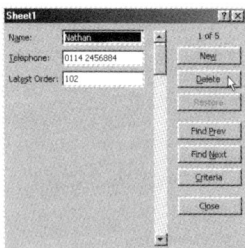

Figure 8.3 The Delete command button in the Form dialog box.

Finding a file

To find a file, you can use Form or the database.

Find with Form:

1. Click anywhere on your database.
2. Select Data and then Form.
3. Click Criteria.
4. Enter the conditions you want; for example, the command in 451F.
5. Click Next to confirm.

   Your file is automatically displayed *in full*.

Find from a database:

Let us assume that your database includes several hundreds of names. To find the file named 'James':

1. Open the Edit menu.
2. Select the Find option.
3. Type in the text area the name James.
4. Confirm.

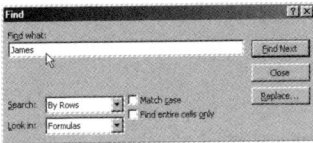

Figure 8.4 Choose the name you wish to find in the Find dialog box.

Criteria

The Criteria command in the Form dialog box finds entries in accordance with the specified conditions.

To scroll through entries, use the directional arrows in the dialog box.

To move by 10 entries at a time, click on the scrollbar between the arrows.

■ Moving within a database

To move within the database, you have two commands at your disposal:

- **The Find Prev command** displays the previous entry in a list. If you specify a condition with the Criteria button, Find Prev displays the previous entry in accordance with the specified condition.

- **The Find Next command** displays the next entry in a list. If you specify a condition with the Criteria button, Find Next displays the next entry in accordance with the specified condition.

■ Sorting a database

The Name field

You can sort your database according to alphabetical criteria.

1. Select your database.
2. Click the Data menu.
3. Select the Sort option.

Select Sort by name in ascending order.

Your list of names is sorted by alphabetical order.

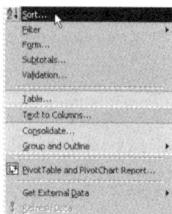

Figure 8.5 The Sort option in the Data menu.

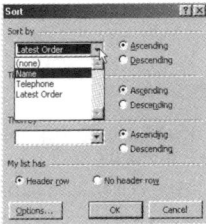

Figure 8.6 The dialog box which allows you to sort your list in alphabetical order.

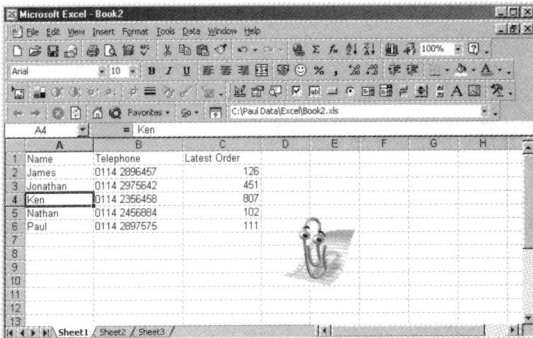

Figure 8.7 Your list is sorted by ascending alphabetical order.

You can apply Sort to a small selection rather than to the whole list.

For this simply select a few names you wish to sort and select Sort in the Data menu.

The Last command

To implement sort with commands:

1. Select your database.

2. Open the Data menu.

3. Select the Sort option.

4. Click Last in the text box.

5. Confirm by clicking on OK.

Your list is sorted by ascending order of importance for the last command.

Figure 8.8 Sort your list using commands.

■ Using filters

AutoFilter

AutoFilter displays only rows corresponding to the value of the cell active, and inserts AutoFilter arrows to the right of each column label.

To activate AutoFilter:

1. Select the Data menu.

2. Select the Filter submenu.

3. Confirm.

To deactivate AutoFilter and restore the whole list:

1. Select the Data menu.

2. Select the Filter submenu.

3. Click the AutoFilter tick box.

You can also select the Show All option.

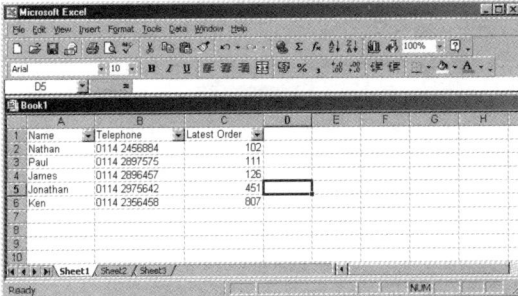

Figure 8.9 AutoFilter is active.

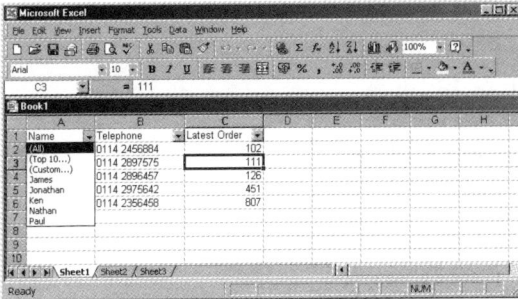

Figure 8.10 How to use AutoFilter.

Advanced Filter

The Advanced Filter filters data in a sorted list which is displayed in the rows meeting a condition specified with a range of conditions.

The Advanced Filter allows you to implement a more complex selection on the basis of different conditions applied to a single column. You can apply three conditions to the Name column, for example.

To get Advanced Filter:

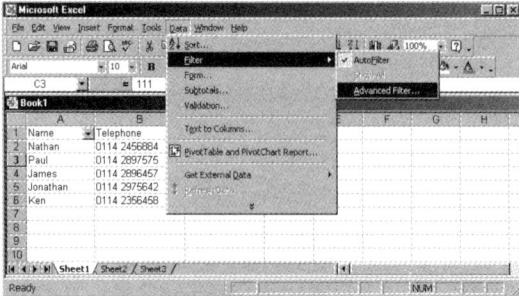

Figure 8.11 Selecting Advanced Filter.

1. Open the Data menu.
2. Select the Filter submenu.
3. Select Advanced Filter.

Extracting a file with AutoFilter

To extract a file:

1. Click anywhere in your database.
2. Open the Data menu.
3. Click the Filter submenu.
4. Select AutoFilter.

The AutoFilter may already be activated.

On your database there are now three drop-down menus, indicated by a small black down arrow each corresponding to one of the three records.

Select the name of the client which corresponds to the file you wish to extract.

1. Open the Name menu.
2. Select 'James'.
3. Confirm.

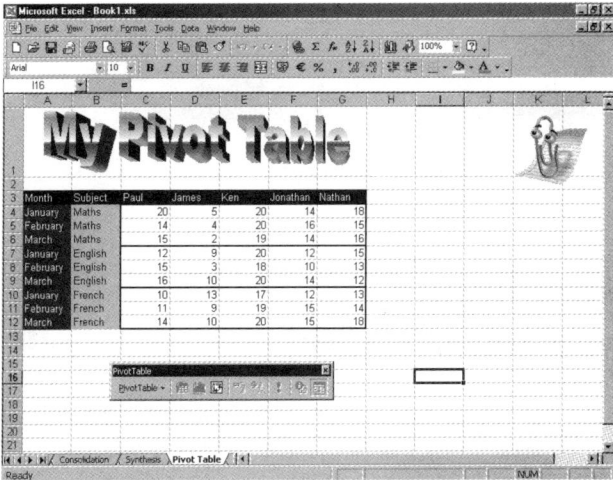

Figure 8.12 Only the James file is automatically displayed.

Your database is filtered. Only the extracted file 'James' is automatically displayed.

To display the whole of your list:

1. Open the Data menu.
2. Select Filter.
3. Click Show All.

Extracting a file with Advanced Filter

The Advanced Filter works in a different way. It uses one or several conditions rows, which allow you to set limits, in order to obtain files on the basis of complex conditions.

To implement a complex filter, fill the dialog box as follows:

- **List Range** defines the database.
- **Criteria range** must go before the database.
- **Copy to** defines the address for placing the files.

■■

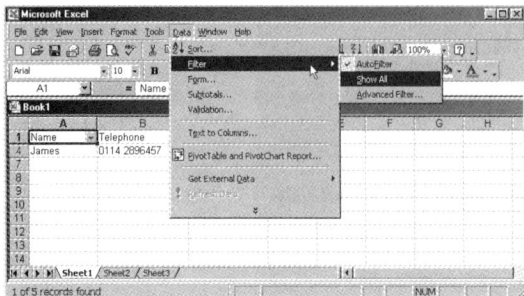

Figure 8.13 The Show All option allows you to view the whole of your list.

In the example in Figure 8.14, the question is 'Which files have a Latest Order over 200'. The answer is two files, and is provided in the receiving area.

Figure 8.14 Selecting one or several empty rows to specify conditions.

Caution, the areas must all be selected before posing the request with the Data menu/Filter/Advanced Filter. The areas must be sufficiently large. Apply a large size.

The subtleties and the actual difficulties of advanced filters cannot be covered in a book in this series. If you wish to learn more about this subject, refer to other Pearson publications which are meant for advanced users and specialists.

Operators

Operators which are allowed for filtering entries are:

- The 'equal' sign (=) returns exact correspondences.
- The 'greater than' sign (>) returns higher values.
- The 'less than' sign (<) returns lower values.
- The 'greater than or equal to' sign (>=) returns higher or equal values.
- The 'less than or equal to' sign (<=) returns higher or equal values.
- The 'not equal to' sign (<>) returns different values.
- The 'equal' sign (=) by itself finds all the empty fields.
- The 'not equal to' sign (< >) by itself finds all the empty fields.
- The Clear operator removes all conditions.

9 Creating a chart

■ Charts

Excel 2000 has considerably improved its chart function. Creating visually impressive charts in Excel can now be done by almost anyone. As well as standard charts, you can now add radar, cylinders, pyramids and bubbles to your tables. And, obviously, all these geometrical shapes are in 3D.

One of the most spectacular enhancements in the latest Excel 2000 version is the ability to rotate charts and legends from 0° to 180°.

Chart production has become an integral part of the electronic office, just as much as text handling or accountancy packages. Charts are used in documents and accountancy reports to provide higher-impact advertising messages, company reports, year-end accounts and balance sheets.

Charts are visually appealing and make it easy for users to see comparisons, patterns and trends in data.

To create a chart, you must first enter the data for the chart on the worksheet. Then select the data and use the Chart Wizard to guide you through the process of choosing the chart type and the various chart options.

Before we go on to actually producing a chart appropriate to your data type, let us explain the various tools at your disposal for chart production.

The Chart toolbar

The Chart toolbar includes a number of different pop down menus and icons:

- **Chart Type.** Changes the chart type for a single data series, for a group of charts or for a whole chart.
- **Source Data.** Adds or modifies the data series in a chart or selected data references.

- **Chart Options.** Modifies the standard options for the selected chart type. You can rename charts, change their default settings for gridlines and axis and modify the display for data labels.

- **Location.** Organises the position of the selected objects in your worksheet.

- **Add Data.** Adds data series or selected data references to the chart.

- **Add Trendline.** Adds trendlines or modifies the trendline type in data series in unstacked 2D area, bar, column, line stock, scatter and bubble charts.

- **3D View.** Controls the display angle from the 3D chart. A sample chart, displayed in the dialog box, shows the current settings.

- **Auto scaling.** Determines whether the size of the worksheet chart is or isn't independent of the window size. A created worksheet chart is automatically independent of the window size.

- **Chart Window.** Displays or hides the chart window.

- **Titles.** Formats the chart title. The available formatting options vary according to the selected chart element. If you select a legend, the option becomes selected legend.

- **Chart Wizard.** The Chart Wizard will guide you step by step in the creation of your charts. You will be able to create high quality charts following the four steps indicated.

- **Chart Types.** Column, bars, line, pies, scatter, area, doughnut, radar, surface, bubble, stock, cylinder, cone, pyramid.

- **Vertical gridlines.** Displays or hides the vertical gridlines in the chart.

- **Horizontal gridlines.** Displays or hides the horizontal gridlines in the chart.

- **Legend.** This command adds a legend to the right of the plot area or resizes it. Clicking on this command deletes the existing legend.

- **Data Table.** Displays values for each data series in a table positioned underneath the chart.
- **By Row.** Plots data series in the chart row by row.
- **By Column.** Plots data series in the chart column by column.

Which chart type do I choose?

There are six main chart types:

- **Lines.** These are used for indicating an evolving situation. Example: sales for the first quarter.

- **Surface.** Shows trends in values across two dimensions in a continuous curve. They allow a good comparison of two different values. Surface charts are very useful to highlight the magnitude of an evolution. Example: the realised profit month by month for the last year.

- **Vertical Bar.** Vertical bars, also called 'Histograms' or 'Columns'. They compare values across categories. Example: variations over several years for employees, days off and salaries. Stacked columns are a variant of clustered columns as they compare the contribution of each value to a total across categories. Example: the contribution of the sale price, or the breakdown by types of articles to the total. 100% stacked columns compare the percentage each value contributes to a total across categories.

Do not underestimate vertical bar charts, or histograms! They can be very useful. If, for example, in an examination situation in which you are unsure as to which type of chart would be best suited to your case study, vertical bar charts are a perfect solution!

- **Pie chart.** Displays the contribution of each value to a total. It is also used to show a split value. Example: sales for a company split by geographical area.

- **Scatter.** Scatter charts or 'XY charts' compare pairs of values, highlighting the cause-effect relationship. Example: advertising costs and increase in sales.

- **Custom Types.** Stock exchange, timescale pyramids, and so on.

A number of chart types can be combined. A single chart will plot multiple and different data. Example: if you superimpose a histogram on a line chart you can highlight the outcome of a specific series, the best or worst sales results for the year. Always be careful not to overload your charts with data. A surplus of data can cause the message to become blurred.

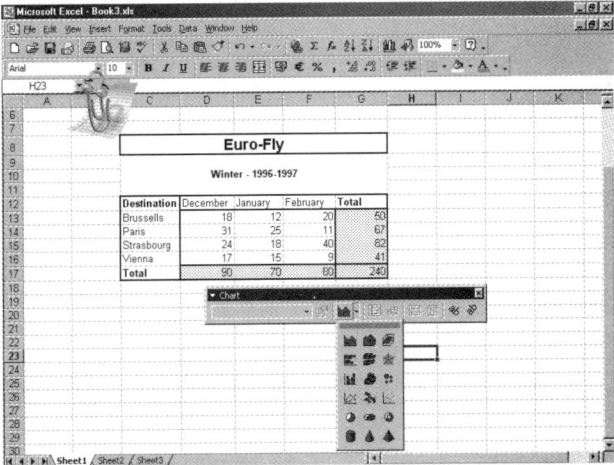

Figure 9.1 The Chart toolbar.

3D charts

Now you have a choice of creating a chart either in 3D or in 2D. 3D charts are very interesting, as well as being more appealing, because they are a better representation of reality.

3D charts, (three-dimensional charts) allow you to represent several series at the same time in perspective. In 3D charts, Z is the vertical axis. The data name is always plotted along the X axis, but the series name is plotted along Y and the values are listed along the Z axis.

A histogram for the Euro Fly company

The Euro Fly company sells air tickets for European destinations. You wish to chart sales of tickets by month and by destination. The period you are most interested in is winter 1996–97, in this case December 1996, January 1997 and February 1997. The destinations are Brussels, Paris, Strasbourg and Vienna.

Which type of chart should you choose to illustrate this case study?

The best solution is an histogram because, in this relatively simple case study, you really need to compare values across categories.

To create a chart, you must select the data you wish to include in the chart. Select the whole of the Euro Fly sheet apart from totals.

Click the Chart Wizard icon in the Standard toolbar.

First Step

You will see a dialog box with a menu. The first tab will offer a set of chart types and chart sub-types, and the second a set of custom charts.

A simple histogram is the chart which is best suited to your data. Click Next.

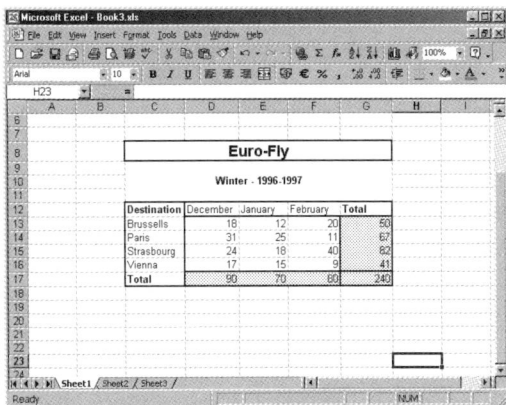

Figure 9.2 Your data before you create a chart.

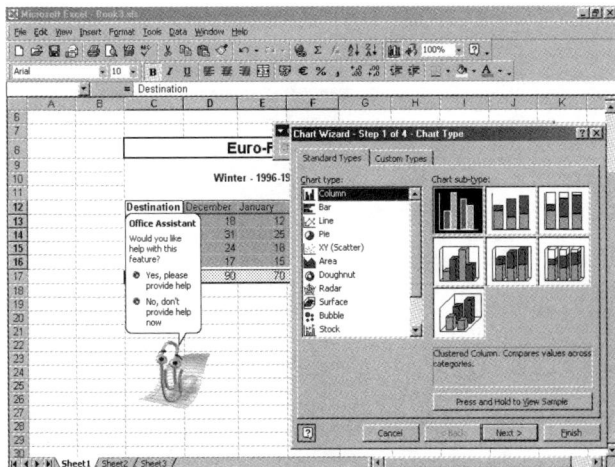

Figure 9.3 Choose the column type.

Second Step

Your data range proposes series by rows or by columns. Choose the series by columns which you think is easier to read. Click Next.

Third Step

You now have a range of options aimed at making your chart even more attractive.

- titles;
- axis;
- gridlines;
- legend.

Enter the title Winter 96-97 and click Next.

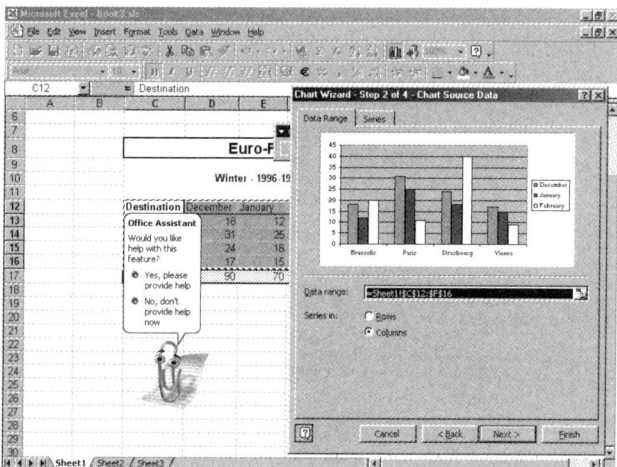

Figure 9.4 Choose the series by columns.

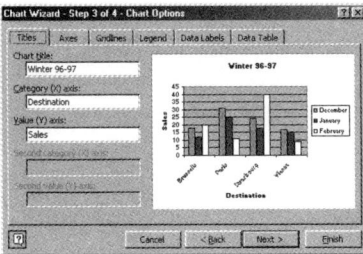

Figure 9.5 Choose your title 'Winter 96-97'.

Fourth Step

Now you have to choose between creating your chart as a new sheet or as an object in the existing worksheet with your data. Tick the As object box in Euro Fly.

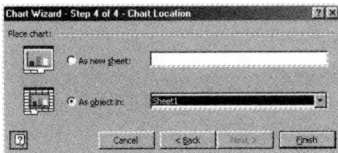

Figure 9.6 Fourth and last step.

Click Finish. Your chart is now placed in your worksheet. Now you only need to adjust the available space in your worksheet. To do this, use the small resizing black arrows located along the edges of the chart.

■ Activating a chart

To activate a chart, double click inside its chart area. The chart area is now surrounded by a border.

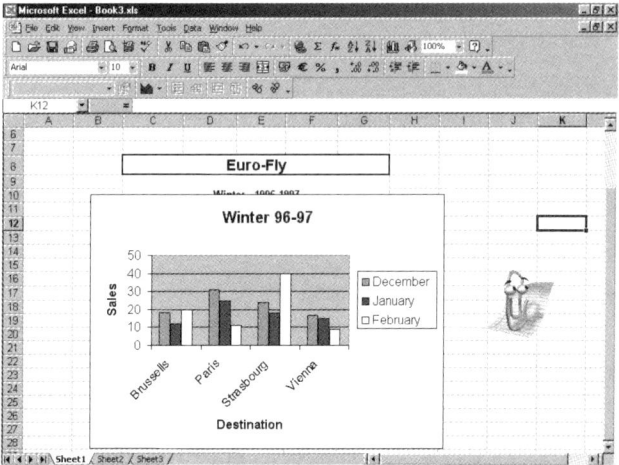

Figure 9.7 Adjust the size of your chart to the available space in your worksheet.

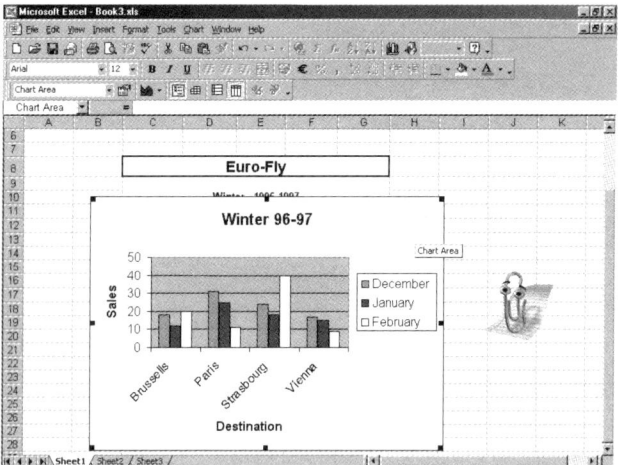

Figure 9.8 To activate your chart, double click on the chart area.

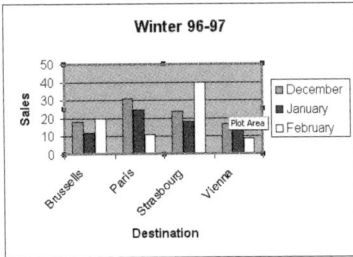

Figure 9.9 To activate your chart title double click it.

■ Modifying a chart

Once your chart has been activated, you can carry out any modifications you require.

For example, you can modify the title font.

Click the chart title; it becomes active immediately.

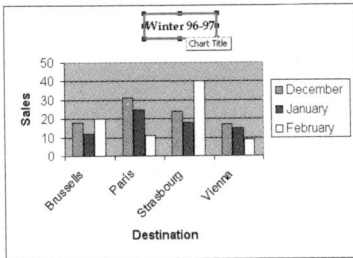

Figure 9.10 Chart Title Format allows you to format your title.

Click the Format chart title icon.

Select the Book Antiqua font and size 12.

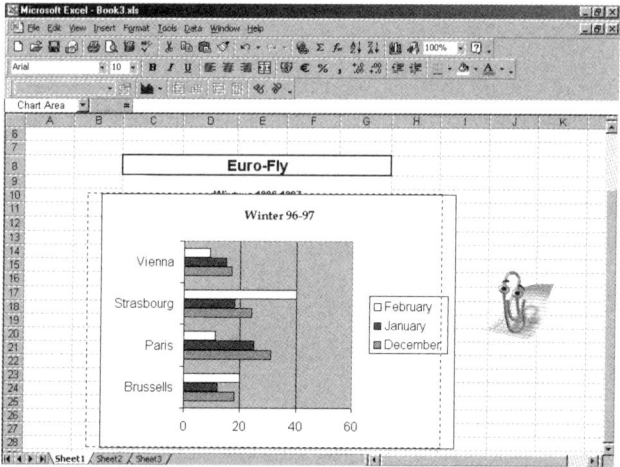

Figure 9.11 Move your chart to the chart area.

■ Modifying a chart type

Do you think that a Histogram chart is not clear enough?

If you prefer a Horizontal Bar chart:

1. Click anywhere on the chart to activate it.
2. Select the Chart Type icon; and you have a selection of eighteen types of chart.
3. Choose a Horizontal Bar chart.

■ Moving a chart

To move a chart:

1. Click anywhere on your chart.
2. Drag it to the required position.

A dotted line indicates the size of your graphic object.

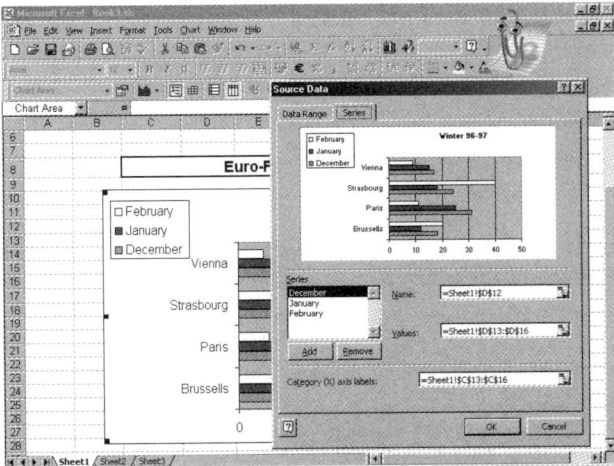

Figure 9.12 The Chart menu with the Source Data option.

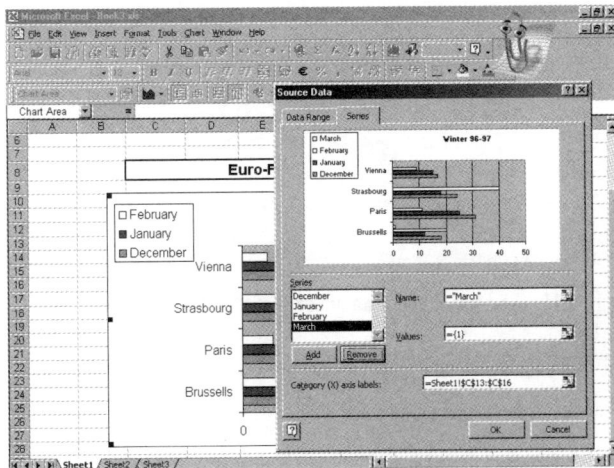

Figure 9.13 Enter the name of the series you wish to add on the
Series tab.

■ Modifying a chart series

To modify a chart series:

1. Click anywhere on your chart to activate it.

2. Open the Chart menu.

3. Select the Source Data submenu.

The Series tab will display a dialog box where you can enter the name of the series you wish to add or delete.

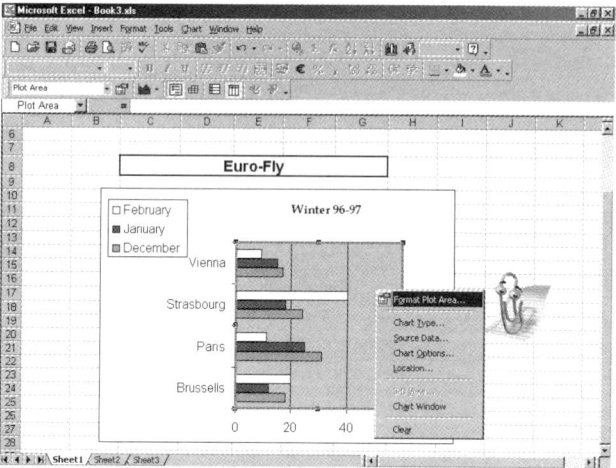

Figure 9.14 The Format plot area dialog box allows you to format your chart.

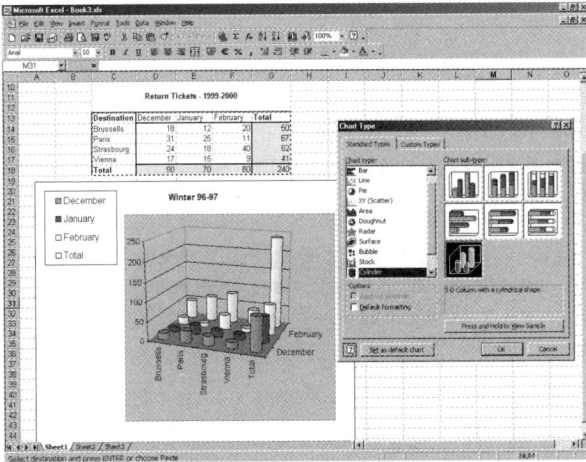

Figure 9.15 Your 3D chart!

■ Formatting a chart

Simple formatting

To implement a simple formatting for a chart, this is what you do:

1. Click anywhere on your chart to activate it.

2. Select the Format icon from the plot area. This icon changes its function (Format Chart Area, Format Plot Area, Format Chart Title) according to where you are in the chart when clicking on it.

3. Choose a colour which is not too aggressive, in line with Euro Fly's corporate image as a background for the chart area.

While you are at it, you can also add a shadow to your title:

1. Click on it to activate it.
2. Click the Format chart title icon.
3. Choose a Custom border and a shadow for your title. You can also choose a colour, a weight, and various fill effects for your title.

Avoid using red when formatting figures. This colour has a negative connotation. Try instead to use colours which match the company's corporate image and logo to create a coherent look for your charts.

3D formatting

Why not use 3D charts, since we now have the opportunity? Thanks to the drawing facilities in your software and to ever more sophisticated chart functions, users and above all end users of tables are becoming more and more demanding. Do not hesitate to present your chart in the best possible way, always keeping in mind that your tables must be as easy to read as you can possibly make them.

1. Click anywhere on your chart.
2. Select Chart Wizard.
3. Select Cylinder.
4. Click Finish to confirm.
5. Click the corners of your new chart to tilt it.

10
Creating
a macro

Some tasks are repetitive and always require the same sequence of actions. To automate a task you perform frequently, you can create a specific worksheet, known as a worksheet macro. This macro must include all the steps you take when you perform a series of commands, in order of execution. You can assign the macro to a toolbar button.

■ Creating a macro

The macro tools

Before you can create your own macros, you must get acquainted with the macro tools available in Excel.

In the Tools menu you will find the Macro option and Additional Controls.

The Macro option

The Macro option displays the Macro dialog box.

In this dialog box there are drop-down lists and the following commands:

- **Macro Name.** The Macro name box allows you to type the name for the macro you wish to create, modify or delete, or for which you wish to define options.

- **Run.** The Run command runs the selected macro. If a macro contains arguments (variables), it cannot be run from the Macro dialog box.

- **Step Into.** The Step Into command runs the code of the selected macro one line of code at a time.

- **Edit.** The Edit command opens the selected macro in the Visual Basic Editor, the collection of dialog boxes for creating macros, and for debugging macros. You are now in Visual Basic programming mode.

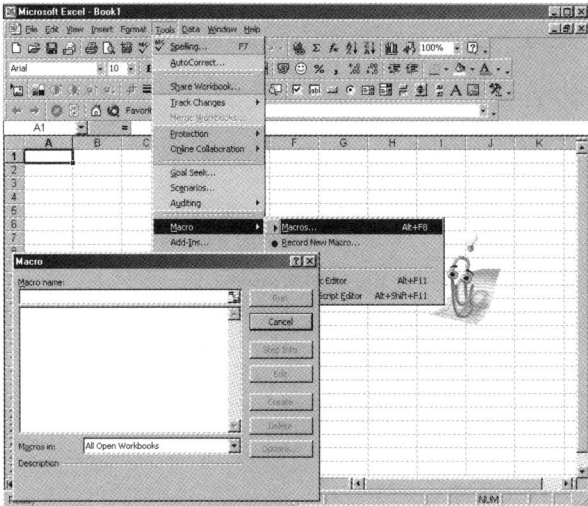

Figure 10.1 The Macro dialog box in the Tools menu.

- **Create.** The Create command opens a new module in the Visual Basic Editor so that you can create a new macro. This command button is only available if you have entered a new name in the Macro name box.

- **Delete.** Deletes the selected macro.

- **Options.** The Options command button opens a new dialog box which assigns a keyboard shortcut to the selected macro, which is Ctrl+the letter you type.

- **VBAProject Properties.** The various text boxes allow you to add notes on the macro which simplifies its use.

Complementary macro options

This option includes:

- A drop-down list containing programs available in Excel, which are advanced macros and complete programs at the

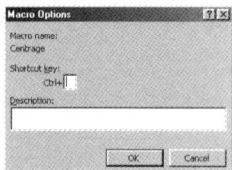

Figure 10.2 The Macro Options dialog box.

same time. The best known is Solver. It solves equations according to set conditions. For example, how can I spend more and earn less? The Solver does not simply find answers, but, in this example, it will be realistic enough to tell you that there is really no solution to your problem.

■ An Office Assistant for file conversion.

Simply tick a check box to load a complementary macro and to run it in Excel. If you want to remove a complementary macro and free up some memory, deactivate the check box.

■ Recording a macro

Before recording a macro, it is strongly recommended that you prepare it properly and plan the various steps very carefully. In practice, if you make even the tiniest error when registering a macro, the corrections you have made are also recorded.

Do not confuse running a macro with recording a macro. Recording a macro allows you to create the macro which means indicating its various actions to Excel. Running a macro consists simply in launching it.

First example

1. Open the Tools menu.
2. Select Macro.

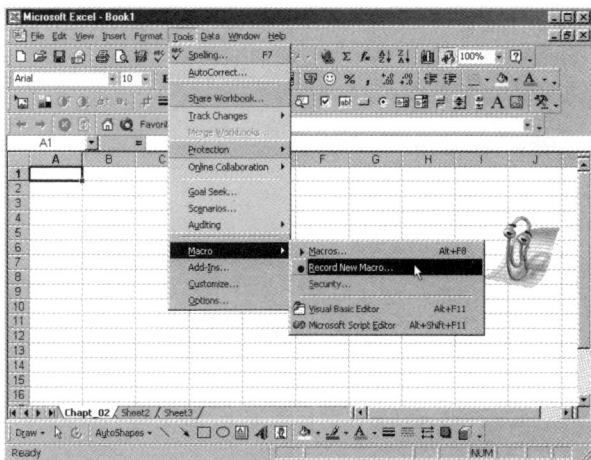

Figure 10.3 Recording a new Macro.

3. Click Record New Macro.

4. Choose the name you wish to assign to your macro in the text box in the dialog box.

5. Confirm by clicking OK. Choose a short name, preferably, and one that contains only letters.

6. Execute the operations for creating your macro.

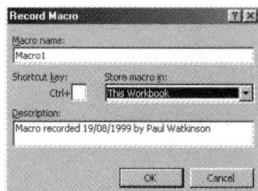

Figure 10.4 Creating a Macro with the default name.

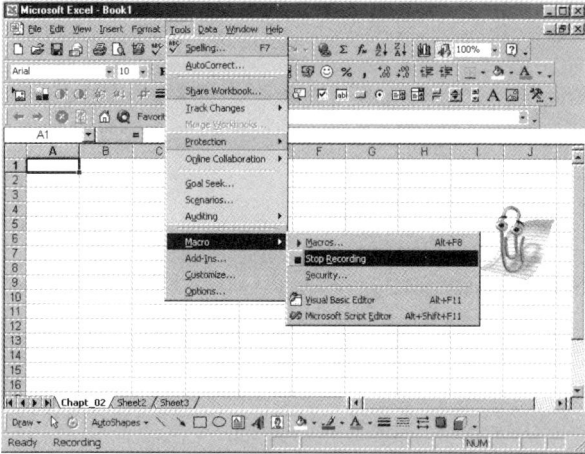

Figure 10.5 The Stop Recording option.

7. Open the Tools menu.

8. Click on the Macro submenu.

9. Select the Stop Recording option.

Your macro is complete.

To stop a macro before completion, press Esc.

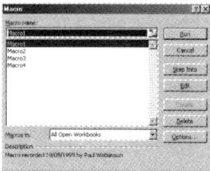

Figure 10.6 Running a Macro.

Second example

To get better acquainted with the creation of macro commands, you will create a general macro. The macro will be used to centre a worksheet title or the title of one of its paragraphs horizontally, vertically and on several columns (by merging cells).

Proceed as follows:

1. Write your text. In this example, this will be My Perfectly Centred Title.

2. Starting from the text cell, select the whole of the area over which to centre the text.

3. Starting from here, click Tools, Macro, Record New Macro.

   a. Call the macro Centre_1.

   b. Add it to the Personal Macro Workbook, so that it is available for general use.

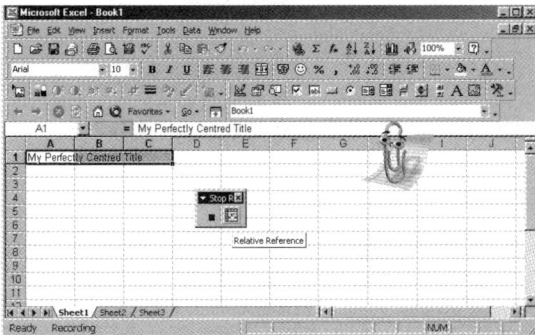

Figure 10.7 Entering text to be handled by the macro.

4. Confirm. The macro recording symbol is automatically displayed, with its two buttons:

   ■ Relative reference.

   ■ Close.

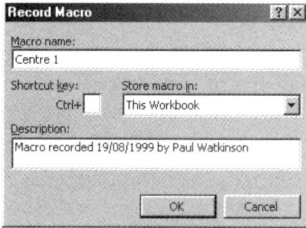

Figure 10.8 Naming your macro.

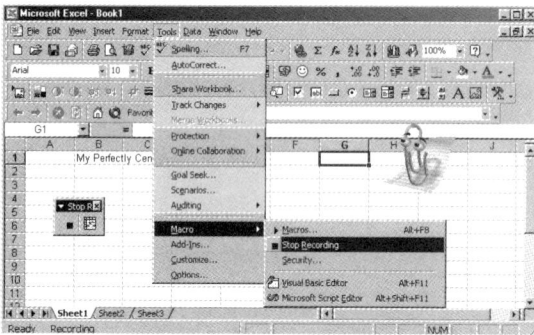

Figure 10.9 The Relative reference button in the Macro toolbar.

1. Click Format, Cells.
2. Select the Alignment tab.
3. Select Center both in the Horizontal and Vertical box.
4. Go back to your row.
5. Tick the Merge cells check box.
6. Confirm. The text is automatically displayed as centred, as previewed.
7. Click the Stop button (the first of the two).

Assigning a command name to a macro

1. Click with the right mouse button on a toolbar.

    Instead of activating a command, this operation displays a drop-down menu.

2. Select Customize.

3. Choose the Commands tab.

4. Click Macros.

5. Place the Custom Button on the toolbar.

6. Click with the right mouse button on the *smiley* (the smile button).

7. Select the Edit button.

8. Modify the Centre button.

9. Assign it a command name which is automatically displayed in the info balloon.

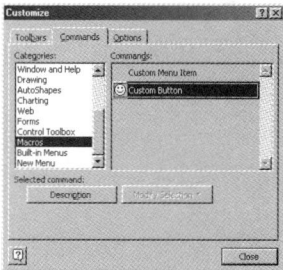

Figure 10.10 Drag and drop the custom button (Smiley) on one of the toolbars, where you wish it to be placed.

10. Close the windows you no longer need.

11. Click the New button.

12. In the dialog box which is automatically displayed, select the Centre_1 macro.

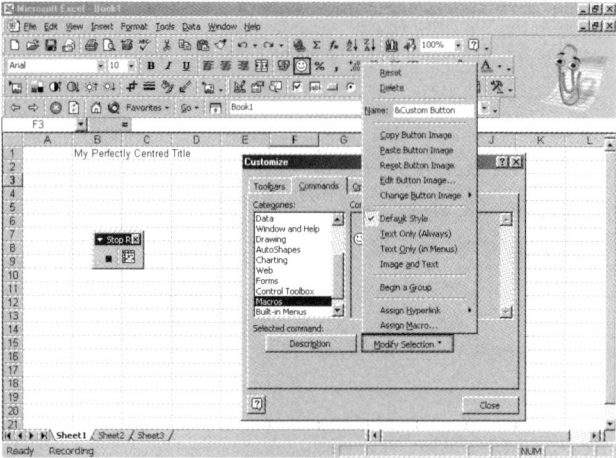

Figure 10.11 Record the Name area, then assign a macro.

The new tool is now ready to work. It is effective, clear and functional.

You can test it.

1. Choose a title for your invention.
2. Select it.
3. Click your Centre macro.
4. Launch the macro.

Your title is centred.

For a macro to be able to select a specific cell, execute an action, then select another cell correlated with the active cell, mix absolute and relative when you register it.

The Relative reference option allows you to register a macro using relative references.

If you do not click on the Relative reference option, you can record a macro with absolute references.

■ Viewing a macro

To view a macro:

1. Open the Tools menu.
2. Select the Macro submenu.
3. Click the Macros option.
4. Click the Step into button.

You can now view the detailed operations of your macro.

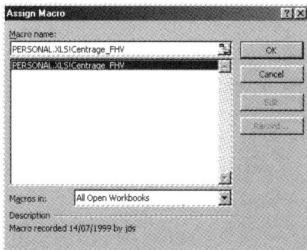

Figure 10.12 Select the macro you have chosen. This will be linked to the newly inserted icon.

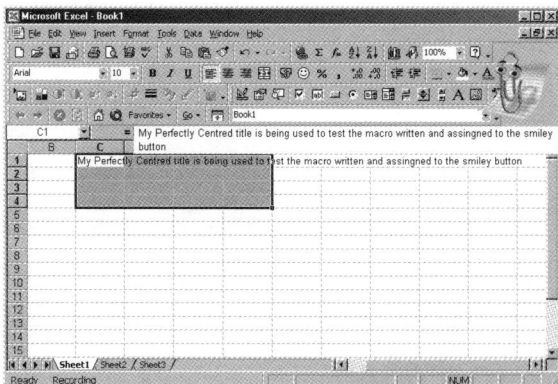

Figure 10.13 To test your macro, write a longer sentence.

■ Copying a macro

The syntax of your first macro may well include commands which you want to assign to another macro. You can copy all or part of your first macro into another. You can also copy a macro form to duplicate all the macros which are included.

Copying part of a macro

To copy part of a macro:

1. Open the Tools menu.
2. Click Macro.
3. Choose the name of the macro to be copied in the Name area.
4. Click Modify.
5. Select the parts of the macro you wish to copy.

If you wish to copy it all, you must include the Sub and End Sub rows in the selection.

1. Click Copy.
2. Open the form where you wish to insert this copy.
3. Click Paste.

Copying a macro form

1. Open the Tools menu.
2. Click Macro.
3. Choose the name of the macro to be copied in the Name area.
4. Click Modify.
5. Select Macros in the Tools menu.
6. Click Visual Basic Editor.

7. Open the Visual Basic Editor View menu.

8. Click the Project Explorer option.

9. Drag the form you wish to use.

10. Copy into the destination workbook.

■ Modifying a macro

You have made a syntax error in your macro. You wish to correct it.

1. Open the Tools menu.

2. Click the Macro option.

3. Select Modify.

The syntax of your macro will now be displayed and you can modify it as you wish.

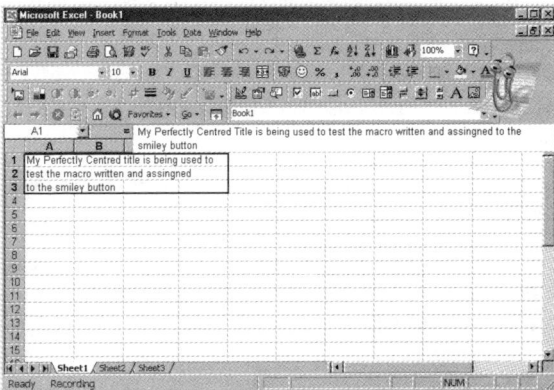

Figure 10.14 The new tool behaves like a command.

■ Assigning a macro to a toolbar button

1. Open the View menu.
2. Select the Toolbars submenu.
3. Select the Customize option.
4. Click the Commands tab.
5. Select the Macros option.

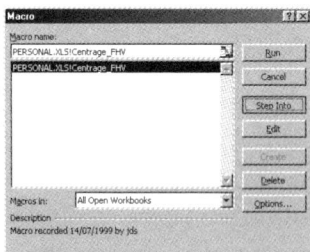

Figure 10.15 **The command button Step Into to view the selected macro**.

6. Click Custom Menu Item.
7. Drag it to the required position in the toolbar keeping the left mouse button pressed.

The pointer now becomes a white arrow in a small grey rectangular command button.

Now place it in the position you have chosen in the toolbar, releasing the left mouse button. The Custom Menu Item button is now in the toolbar.

■ Modifying the appearance of a macro button

To modify the appearance of your macro button, this is what you do:

1. Open the View menu.
2. Select the Toolbar option.
3. Click Customize.
4. Select your Custom Button.
5. Click Modify Selection.
6. Select the new button image; you can choose from 42 new icons. If you do not like any of these, create your own.
7. Choose the bell, for example.

Your new icon is now placed in the toolbar.

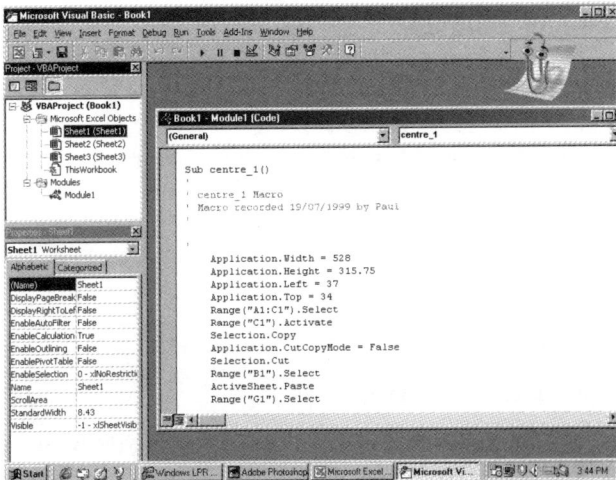

Figure 10.16 Viewing your macro.

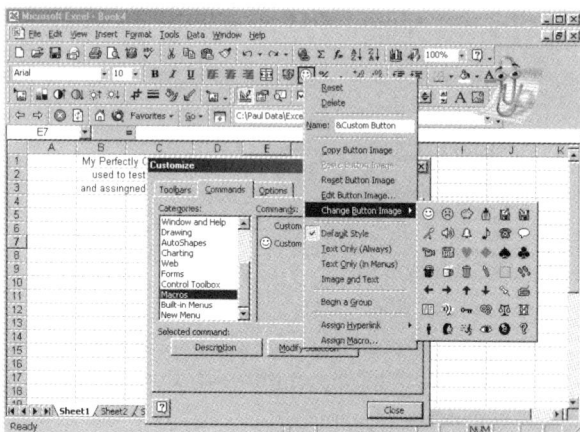

Figure 10.17 Select an icon. Your new icon is placed in the toolbar.

■ Editing a button

You can design your own buttons and make all the alterations you wish.

These are the various operations you must carry out:

1. Open the View menu.
2. Select the Toolbar option.
3. Click Customize.
4. Select your Custom Button.
5. Click Modify selection.
6. Select Edit Button Image.

Use your imagination to make all the changes you want to your button.

Modify the colours for your bell, by clicking on the colour of your choice and then on the icon. The icon will now be the colour of your choice.

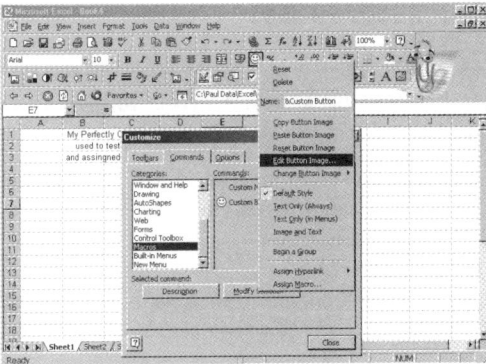

Figure 10.18 The Edit Button Image option allows you to work on your icon.

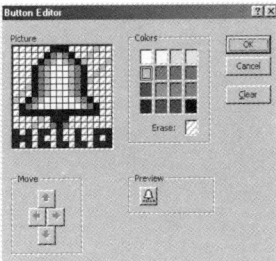

Figure 10.19 The Edit Button Image option allows you to create your icon.

Figure 10.20 Your icon has now been edited.

Once you have completed the operation, click OK. Your modified image returns to its place.

■ Getting rid of macro viruses

There are some viruses which work specifically on macros and which are not detected by Microsoft Excel. You must get antivirus software specifically for macros.

A macro virus is a virus stored in macros. When you execute an action which sets off a macro virus, the virus may activate and place itself in a hidden position.

If you want to know more about macro virus protection, consult the Microsoft website. You can download all the relevant information.

11 Connecting to the Internet

■■■

With Microsoft Office 2000, you can open your workbooks on the Internet. You can publish your own Web pages, view other files with hyperlinks, put your Excel files on the Internet, and search for new data to enhance your work.

For companies, being on the Internet has the advantage of allowing inexpensive long-distance communications and, usually, of avoiding the cost of a dedicated line for data transfer. Since compression programs are currently capable of reducing file sizes at 1 to 20 ratio, the Internet allows quick and efficient data transfer.

■ Selecting the Web toolbar

To select your Web toolbar, do the following:

1. Open the View menu.
2. Click the Toolbar option.
3. Select Customize.
4. Select Web.

The Web toolbar is now displayed.

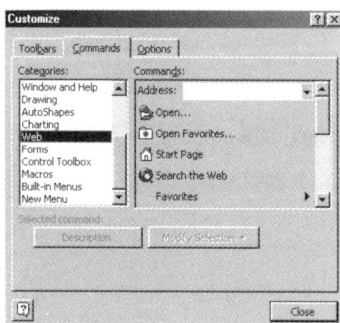

Figure 11.1 The various commands in the Web toolbar.

The Excel Web toolbar allows you to access your Web documents (HTML, Jpeg, Gif and animated Gif format), on the hard disk (offline) as well as from the Web, if you are connected.

It includes the following commands:

- **Address.** In the Address text box, enter the Internet address you wish to call up, or choose an address already in the list.
- **Open.** Opens the hyperlink.
- **Open Favorites.** Displays the folder in the Look in box. The Favorites folder contains shortcuts to currently used files, folders and hyperlinks.
- **Start Page.** You can define the Start Page with the Set Start Page command in the Go menu in the Web toolbar.
- **Search the Web.** Opens a search page on the Web.
- **Go.** Displays a list of commands from the category you select in the Categories area. To add a command in a toolbar, simply drag the item you want from the Commands area to the toolbar.
- **Back.** Opens the previous file in the list containing the last 10 opened files.
- **Stop Current Jump.** Stop the search for the current link.
- **Refresh Current Page.** Refreshes the selected active page.
- **Add to Favorites.** Creates a shortcut to the selected file, folder or link, then it adds it to the Favorites. The original file or folder is in no way affected.
- **Show Only Web Toolbar.** Hides all displayed toolbars apart from the Web toolbar. Simply click again on this button to display the hidden toolbars.
- **Hyperlink.** Inserts or modifies the specific hyperlink.
- **Web Toolbar.** Displays or hides the Web toolbar.

■ Saving a document in HTML format

What is the HTML format?

HTML stands for *Hypertext Markup Language*. It is the file format used on the Web. Used up to now for text formatting, the language has come a long way. It allows you to include sound files, images, video and templates on the sites. HTML is nowadays the standard language for creating Web pages.

An HTML file contains two categories of data:

- **Contents.** The information you want to display on your page. Let us assume that this is a site for displaying the charts you have created. Add some presentation words, your biography and your scanned images.

- **Tags.** Define the format and possible enhancements for the text. In other words, the tags are the programming part of the page. They are invisible.

How to save in HTML format

Click on the File menu, then select Save as Web Page.

Step 1

First select Publish in the Save As dialog box. All your workbook charts have been selected. You can either select a part of your workbook from a predefined set, or you can choose a custom range of cells to publish. To do this, go to the Choose drop-down list and click on it. Select Range of cells. Now, click the box below the drop-down list and you will be taken back to your worksheet. Select the area you want to publish and press the Return key.

Step 2

At this stage, you must give your Web page a title. Do this by clicking Change.

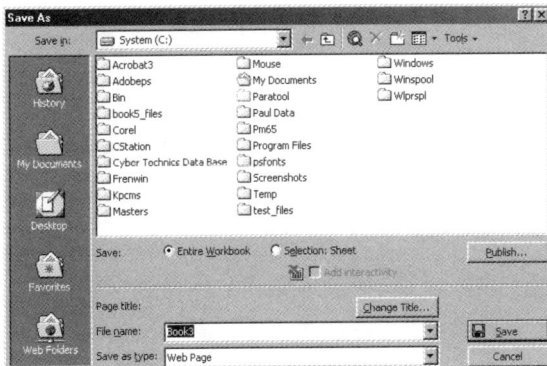

Figure 11.2 The File menu and its Save as Web Page option.

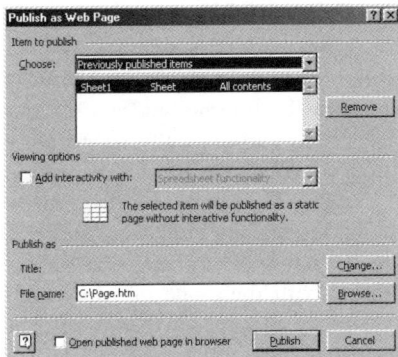

Figure 11.3 Excel converts your data and charts to HTML format.

Step 3

You must now indicate the name and the location of the finished Web page.

Do this by specifying the path of the page in the text box at the bottom of the dialog box. You can save the HTML

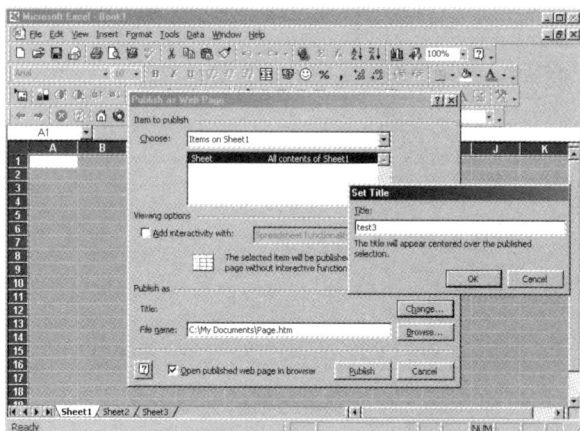

Figure 11.4 Step 2: Type the title for your document.

document on your computer or you can publish it to the Web. This can be done by typing in the Internet address of your page in the text box. Excel will automatically try to place your page at that location (if you have the proper access rights to that particular server). The format of the address should be **http://www.ThisServer.com/MyDocument.html**. Replace 'ThisServer' with the name of your Internet Service Provider and 'MyDocument' with the name of your document. If you have a user name at that server, then it must be typed in between the server address and the name of your document; for example **http://www.freeserve.co.uk/~ko/excel2000.html**. It is also important to remember two things:

- The Internet is case sensitive and you should usually use lower case letters for names of documents.

- The format of a URL varies from one ISP to the next, so check with your ISP before you attempt anything.

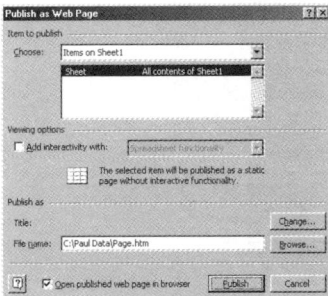

Figure 11.5 The access path for your HTML document is now specified.

■ Displaying a Web page from Netscape Navigator and Internet Explorer

Netscape Navigator and Microsoft Internet Explorer are the most widespread Web browsers available. Between them, they cover approximately 80% of the market. They allow you, among other things, to view World Wide Web pages and to move between them with hypertext links.

Their immediate competitors are Sun's Hotjava Web browser and the European-based Opera. They are similar to Navigator and Internet Explorer but are less successful, relatively speaking, because they came later on to the scene.

You wish to edit the Euro Fly folder from the Internet. You must convert your Euro Fly.xls file into an HTML file.

This is how you do it:

1. Open the File menu.
2. Select Save as Web Page.
3. Click Publish.
4. Select Range of cells in the Choose drop-down list.
5. Select the range to be converted.

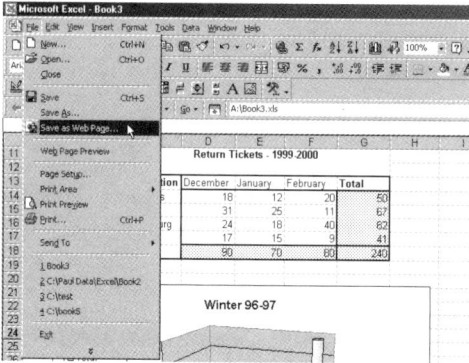

Figure 11.6 To convert your XLS file to HTML format,select the Save As Web Page option in the file menu.

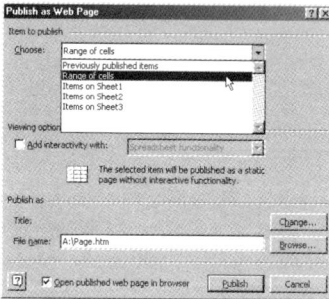

Figure 11.7 The range to be converted to an HTML file.

6. Choose a title for your Web page by clicking Change.

7. Choose the name and location of your HTML document

8. Click the Open Published Web Page in browser check box. This enables you to view the Web page immediately.

   Alternatively you can find the file and double click it.

9. Click Publish.

Publish as Web Page - Range

=Sheet1!Print_Area

Figure 11.8 In the fourth step, the access path for your XLS file converted to an HTML file is automatically displayed.

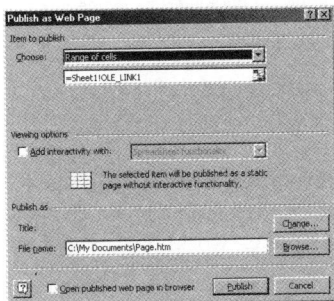

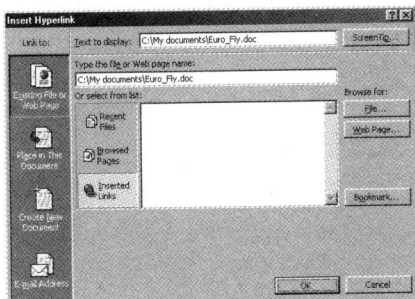

Publish as Web Page

Item to publish

Choose: Range of cells

=Sheet1!OLE_LINK1

Viewing options

☐ Add interactivity with: Spreadsheet functionality

The selected item will be published as a static page without interactive functionality.

Publish as

Title: Change...

File name: C:\My Documents\Page.htm   Browse...

☐ Open published web page in browser   Publish   Cancel

Figure 11.9 In the fourth step, the access path for your XLS file converted to an HTML file is automatically displayed.

Insert Hyperlink

Link to:

Text to display: C:\My documents\Euro_Fly.doc   ScreenTip...

Type the file or Web page name:

C:\My documents\Euro_Fly.doc

Existing File or Web Page

Or select from list: Browse for:

☐ Recent Files   File...

☐ Browsed Pages   Web Page...

Place in This Document

☐ Inserted Links   Bookmark...

Create New Document

E-mail Address

OK   Cancel

Figure 11.10 Your Euro Fly folder opens on the Internet.

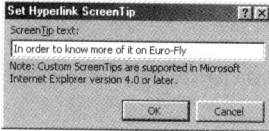

Figure 11.11 Select the ScreenTips option in the Hyperlink dialog box.

■ Creating a hyperlink

What is a hyperlink?

A hyperlink allows you to link different types of data; for example, text and images, and vice versa. It offers a shortcut which gives you fast access to other workbooks and files. Thanks to this method, you can display files which are in your computer or on the Web, which is where you exchange information and view graphics.

To go from one workbook to another, simply click on a link (the address) which is automatically displayed in blue and underlined. When you have finished reading the file, the link changes from blue to mauve.

Creating a hyperlink

Let us imagine that you wish to create a hyperlink to a Word document in a worksheet.

Open the Euro Fly worksheet and the Word document you want to link ('Christmas in Strasbourg').

1. Select the whole Word document 'Christmas in Strasbourg'.
2. Open the Edit menu and select the Copy submenu.
3. Click the Excel Euro Fly document.
4. Click the cell which will contain the hypertext link.

   For our example, use the destination 'Strasbourg' for your Euro Fly table.

5. Click the Edit menu.

6. Select the Paste as Hyperlink submenu.

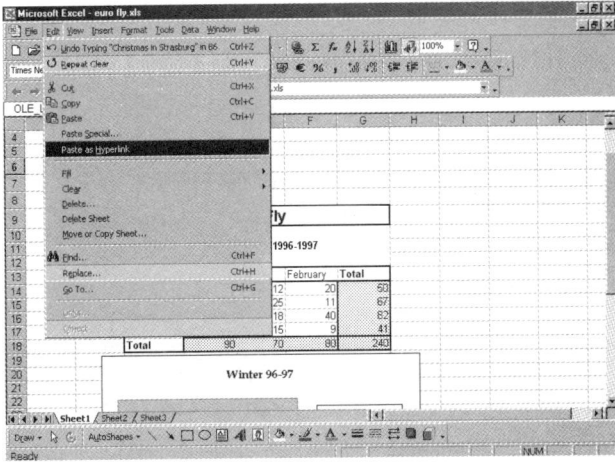

Figure 11.12 Select the Paste as Hyperlink option in the Edit menu.

You will see that the selected text is automatically displayed in the cell containing the link.

The word 'Strasbourg' appears in blue.

To activate the linked text 'Christmas in Strasbourg', simply click on the link when the pointer becomes a small white hand.

When you have completed your consultation, the Strasbourg hyperlink is automatically displayed in mauve.

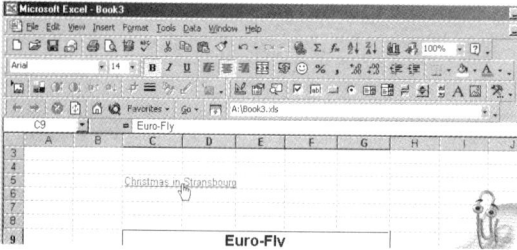

Figure 11.13 Click on the link when your pointer becomes a small white hand.

■ Web surfing

To surf on the Web, you must have a modem which links you to your *provider's* server. Once this connection has been established, simply start your search by keying the address you wish to access in your Internet navigation bar.

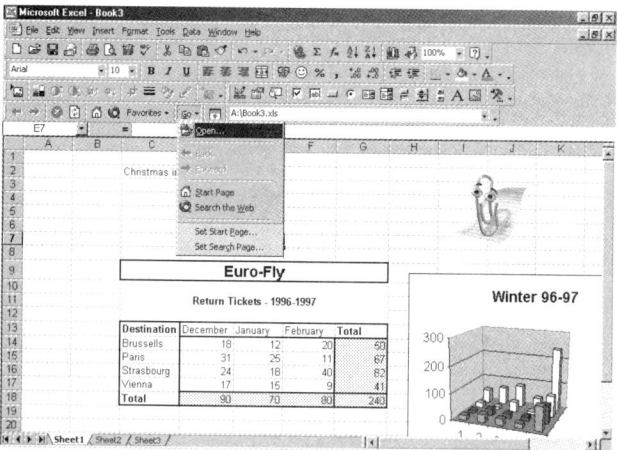

Figure 11.14 The Open option in the Go menu.

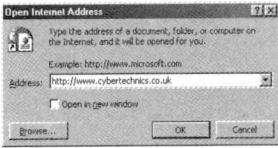

Figure 11.15 Type the address of the Internet site you wish to visit.

To go to a site for which you know the address (URL) from Excel, open the Go menu in the Web toolbar and select Open.

Choose the address of the site to which you wish to go.

You will now get to the website whose address you have entered.

■ Opening Favorites

You have been surfing the Web; you have found a site you like; you 'bookmark' it to add it to the Favorites list. When you want to visit it again, you only need to open the Favorites menu and select the Open Favorites submenu.

The Favorites dialog box will be displayed and you will select, for example, the site **http://www.cybertechnics.co.uk**.

Your site is now in the Favorites list. Whenever you wish to visit it, simply open the Favorites menu and click on it.

■ Going to the Start Page

The Start Page button launches the default Internet connection program, which you have installed on Internet Explorer. The Internet screen appears automatically on the Excel as for a normal session. The opening page is the first to be dis-

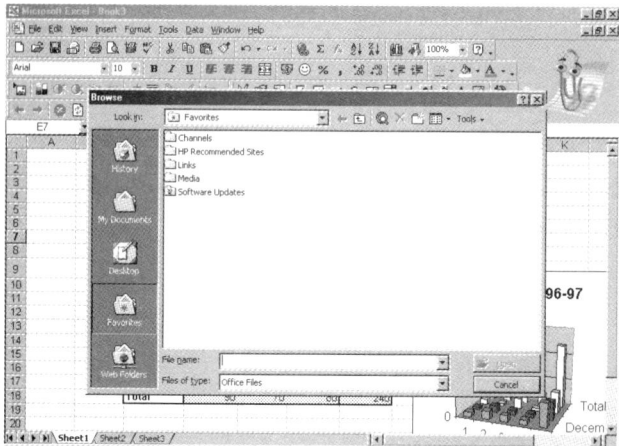

Figure 11.16 Select the Open Favorites option in the Favorites menu.

played. It contains instructions on how to use the Web and the hyperlinks.

You can specify a new Start Page whenever you want:

1. Open the Go menu.

2. Click Set Start Page.

The Start Page dialog box displays the Start Page access path.

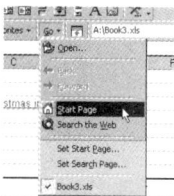

Figure 11.17 The Start Page button.

■ Inserting URLs in your worksheet

To create a hyperlink from your worksheet:

1. Click the check box where you wish to place your Internet address, known as URL (*Uniform Resource Locator*).

2. Open the Insert menu.

3. Select the Hyperlink option.

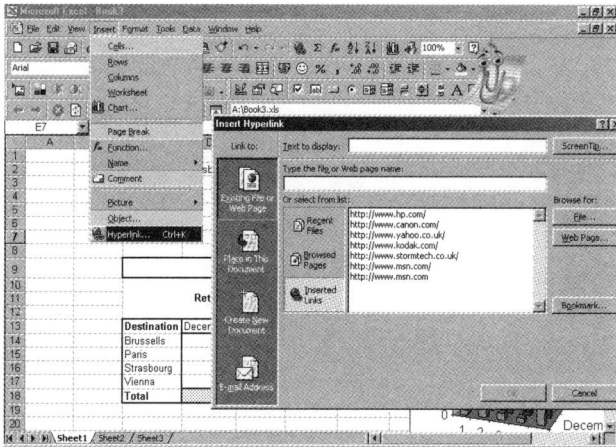

Figure 11.18 The Hyperlink option in the Insert menu.

1. Type your address in the text box.

2. Click the Browse for option in the dialog box.

3. Type the file or Web page name you wish to link to this Internet address.

4. Confirm by clicking OK.

Your URL is now inserted in the selected worksheet. It is blue to distinguish it from other data. Simply click it when your pointer becomes a small white hand. The required site is now displayed.

12 Printing your worksheet

In the default settings, Microsoft Excel 2000 will print the whole worksheet. To print only part of the worksheet, you need to select it. The software has efficient formatting commands, accessed with the File menu and its Page Setup option.

The setup settings are as follows, depending on the printer you have in your configuration:

Page

- **Orientation.** Your worksheet can be printed in Portrait, which means vertically, or Landscape, which means horizontally.

- **Paper size.** This option specifies the paper format.

- **Scaling.** Reduces or enlarges the worksheet, or fits the worksheet to a specific number of pages when you print.

- **Fit to.** Reduces the worksheet or selection when you print so that it fits on the specified number of pages.

Margins

- **Definition.** Specifies Top, Bottom, Left and Right margins.

Be careful that the margins are consistent with the specifications of the headers and footers!

- **Center on page.** Centres the data on the page within the margins by selecting the Vertically check box, the Horizontally check box, or both.

Sheet

- **Row and column headings.** Select this check box to print row numbers and column letters.

- **Gridlines.** Select this check box to print horizontal and vertical gridlines. This option does not affect the screen display.

■ **Comments.** Prints comments either on a separate page (choose At end of sheet) or where you view them on the worksheet (choose As displayed on sheet).

■ Using Print Preview

To print your Euro Fly chart, start by previewing your worksheet. This function allows you to view the layout of your document before going to print.

1. Open the File menu.
2. Select the Print Preview option.

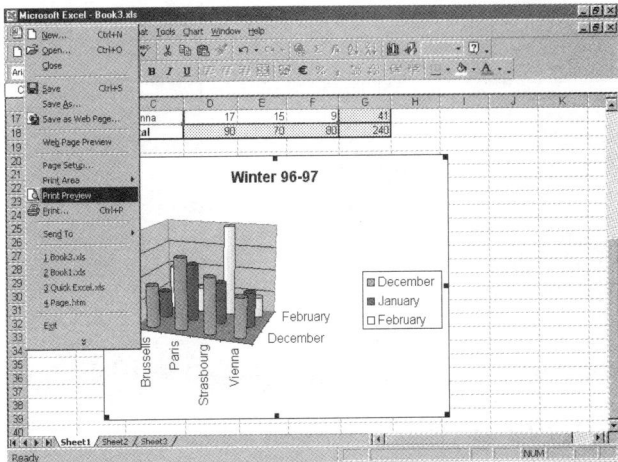

Figure 12.1 Select the Print Preview option in the File menu.

The print preview screen is now displayed with information on Setup, Margins, Page Break Preview, Zoom.

Zoom

On the print preview screen, your pointer changes to a small magnifying glass. If you click with the left mouse button, this small magnifying glass implements the zoom; and your worksheet goes from a full page display to a magnified display. This temporary modification in size does not affect printing. You can toggle between the two views by clicking on any part of the worksheet and going back to the normal Print Preview.

You have positioned the magnifying glass on the chart. The zoom allows you to view all its details.

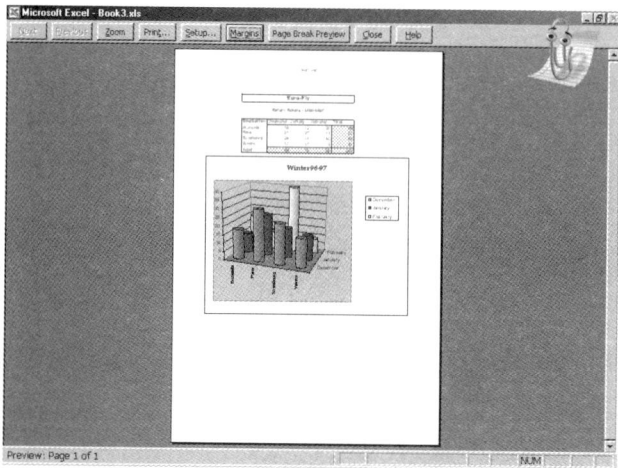

Figure 12.2 The zoom allows you to magnify your view.

To deactivate the zoom option, click on the Zoom button in the Print Preview screen.

Margins

If you click on the Margins button, you will activate the worksheet margins. These will be shown on the screen.

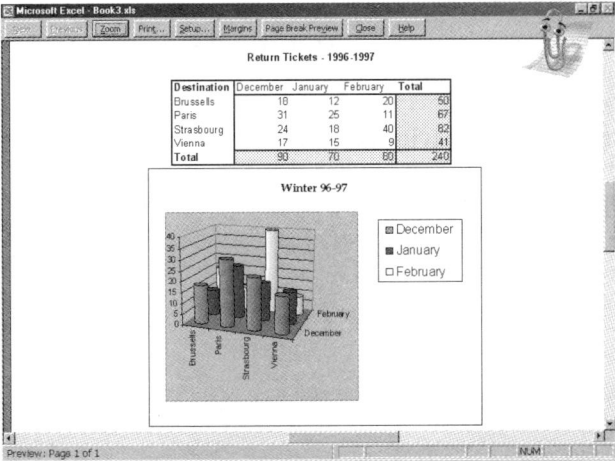

Figure 12.3 The Zoom button in Print Preview

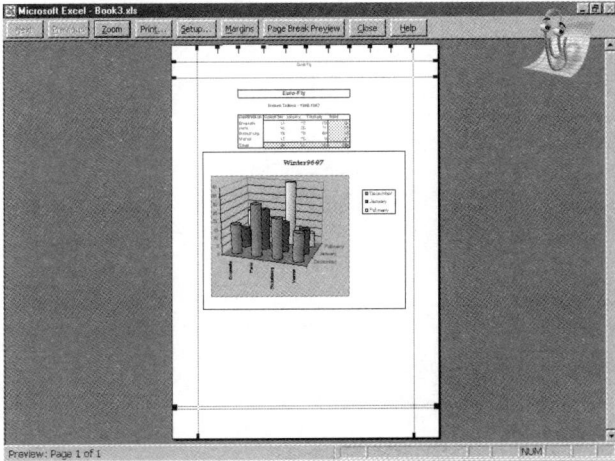

Figure 12.4 The margin resizing arrows in Print Preview.

You can adjust them by dragging your pointer, which changes to two horizontal and vertical black arrows.

■ Defining the print area

With the Define button

Let us assume that you wish to print the sheet only and not the chart. Select your work area and click the Set Print Area button.

Click the Print button or the Print option in the File menu.

Only your work area will be printed.

With the menu

To define a print area with the menu:

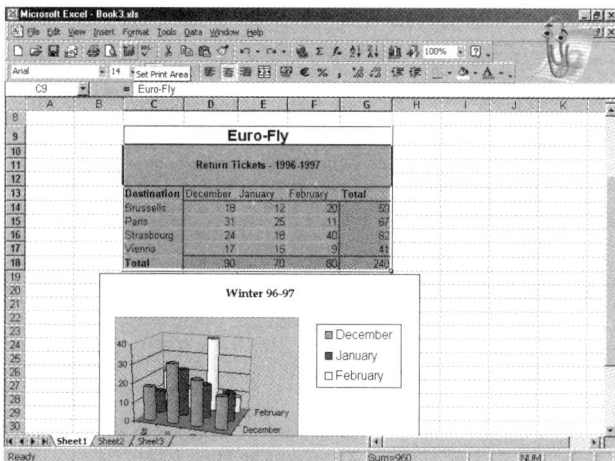

Figure 12.5 Click the Set Print Area button after selecting your work area.

1. Select your work area.
2. Open the File menu.
3. Click the Print Area option.
4. Select Set Print Area.

Only your work area will be printed.

To deselect your print area, this is what you do:

1. Open the File menu.
2. Click the Print Area option.
3. Select Clear Print Area.

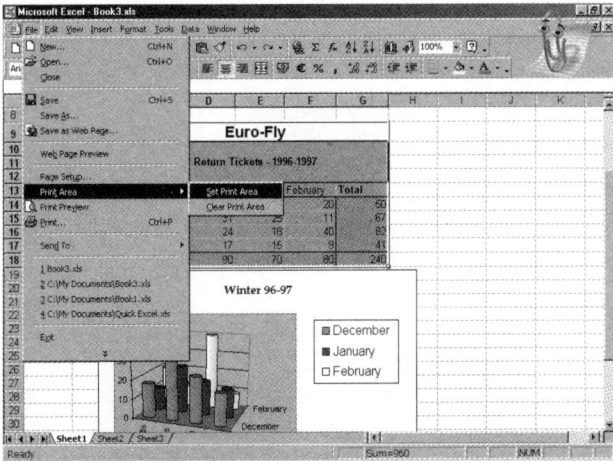

Figure 12.6 The Print Area option in the File menu.

■ Changing the page orientation

Maybe you think that your work area is not oriented properly when you see it printed. It was sent with a 'portrait' orientation (vertical) and you would prefer a 'landscape' orientation (horizontal).

To do this:

1. Select your work area.
2. Open the File menu.
3. Click Page Setup.
4. Select the Page option.

Tick the Landscape check box in the Page tab.

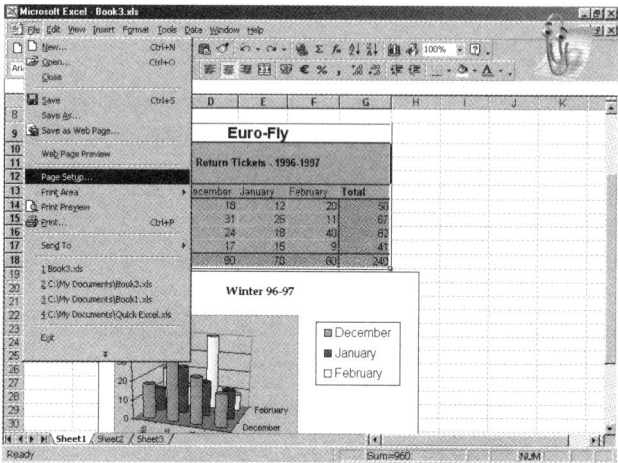

Figure 12.7 Selecting the Page Setup option.

■ Repeating titles on each page

If you have column or row titles, you may wish them to be printed on each page in your worksheet.

1. Open the File menu.

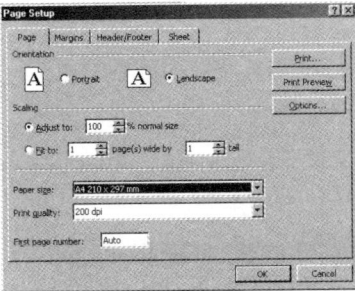

Figure 12.8 The Landscape option: Page tab in the Page Setup dialog box.

2. Select the Page Setup option.

3. Click the Sheet tab.

In the Print titles text area, specify the ones you want to be displayed at the top of columns or rows in your pages.

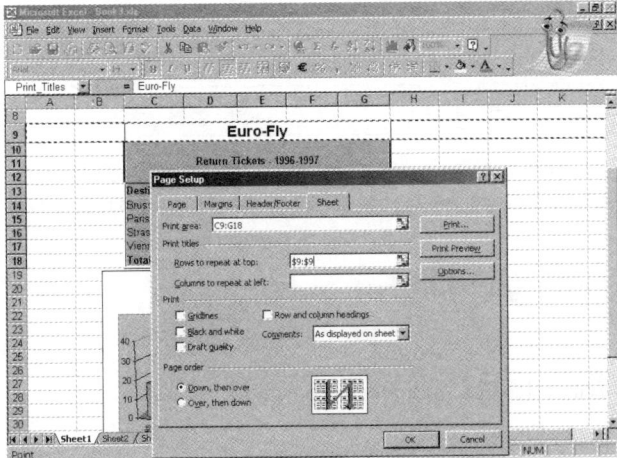

Figure 12.9 Select the Print titles option in the Sheet tab in the Page Setup dialog box.

■ Centring the page

To centre your work area on the page:

1. Click the Margins tab.
2. Click the Horizontally and Vertically check boxes in the Center page option.

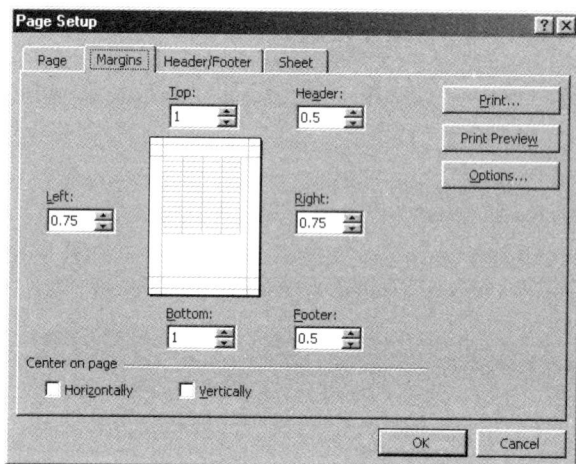

Figure 12.10 To centre margins, click on the Margins tab and define the values for the right, left, top and bottom margins in their respective box.

■ Printing gridlines

1. Open the File menu.
2. Select the Page Setup option.
3. Click the Sheet tab.
4. Tick the Gridlines option in the Print area.

■ Printing in black and white

If you formatted data with colours (underlining, text, chart or border) but you only have a black and white printer, this is what you should do:

1. Open the File menu.
2. Select the Page Setup option.
3. Click the Sheet tab.
4. Tick the Black and white box in the Print area.

With black and white printers, colours are printed in grayscale. To reduce printing time for a colour worksheet, print it in black and white. Excel then prints colours in black and white, and not in grayscale.

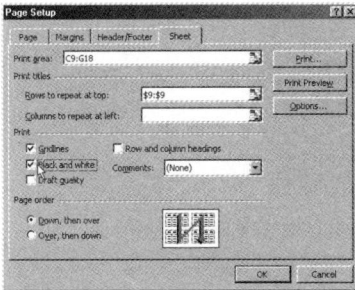

Figure 12.11 The Sheet tab and its Black and white option.

■ Printing comments

At end of sheet

If you wish to print your worksheet with comments:

1. Open the File menu.
2. Select the Page Setup option.

3. Click the Sheet tab.

4. Select At end of sheet in the Comments area.

As displayed on sheet

If you wish to print comments as they are displayed in your worksheet:

1. Open the File menu.

2. Select the Page Setup option.

3. Click the Sheet tab.

4. Select As displayed on sheet in the Comments area.

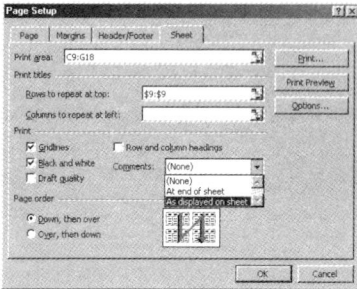

Figure 12.12 As displayed on sheet comments in the Sheet tab.

■ Printing a worksheet on several pages

To print your worksheet on several pages, follow these steps:

1. Open the File menu.

2. Select the Page Setup option.

3. Click the tab Page.

4. Tick the Fit to box.

5. Specify, in number of pages, the width and the height for your printout.

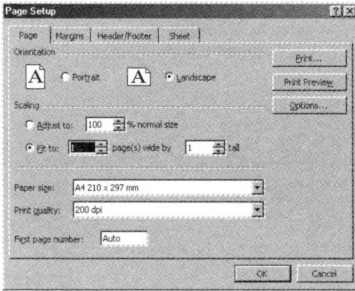

Figure 12.13 Tick the Fit to box.

■ Printing several workbooks at the same time

You can print several workbooks if they are all in the same directory:

1. Open the File menu.
2. Select the Open option.
3. Keep the Ctrl key pressed while you click all the workbooks you wish to print.
4. Click the Tools button.
5. Print.

■ Printing a chart

A chart on the chart sheet

To print a chart on the chart sheet, simply assign a size to it when sending it to print.

██

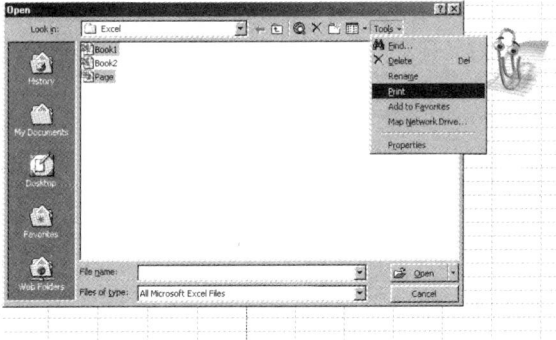

Figure 12.14 The Tools button.

1. Click the chart sheet.
2. Open the File menu.
3. Choose the Page Setup option.
4. Click the Chart tab.
5. In Print chart size, click the required size option.
6. If you click the Custom option, the chart will be printed at the size you specify.

Embedded charts

If your chart is embedded in a worksheet, you need to resize it.

1. Click the chart.
2. Drag the selection handles until you reach the required size.

If you wish to print your embedded chart without the worksheet data, click anywhere on the chart to select it, open Page Setup, choose the Print to file option and click the Chart tab.

■ Printing a specific area in a worksheet

To print a specific area in a worksheet, this is what you do:

1. Open the View menu.
2. Select Page Break Preview.
3. Select the area to be printed.
4. Click with the right mouse button on a selected area.
5. Click Set Print Area in the context menu.

The context menu is the floating menu displayed by clicking an object with the right mouse button.

You can add additional cells to your print area whenever you wish when in Page Break Preview mode. Simply select the cells to be added, click with the right mouse button on a cell in the selection, then select in the context menu the Add to Print Area option.

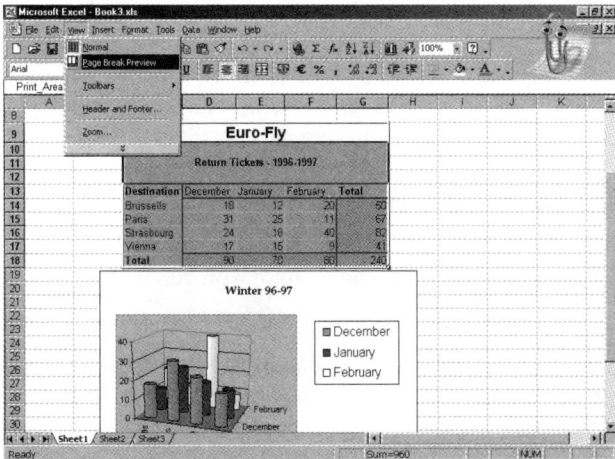

Figure 12.15 The Page Break Preview option in the View menu.

■ Adding headers and footers

Before printing your work area, you can add a header and a footer. You can select predefined templates or create your own.

A worksheet can only have one header and one footer. If you create one, this will automatically replace the default one.

Custom headers and footers
Excel proposes automatic printing of the date and time. To access this:

1. Open the View menu.
2. Select the Header and Footer option.
3. Select the Custom Header option.
4. Write the title of your sheet in the Center section.

   You can choose between Central, Left and Right section. You can use all of them to enter your denominations if you so wish.

5. If you click on the Font, Page Number, Total Pages, Date, Time, File Name and Sheet Name buttons you can customise your headers and footers.

Default headers and footers
To access default headers and footers, do the following:

1. Open the View menu.
2. Select the Header and Footer option.
3. In the Header/Footer box, select the one you prefer.

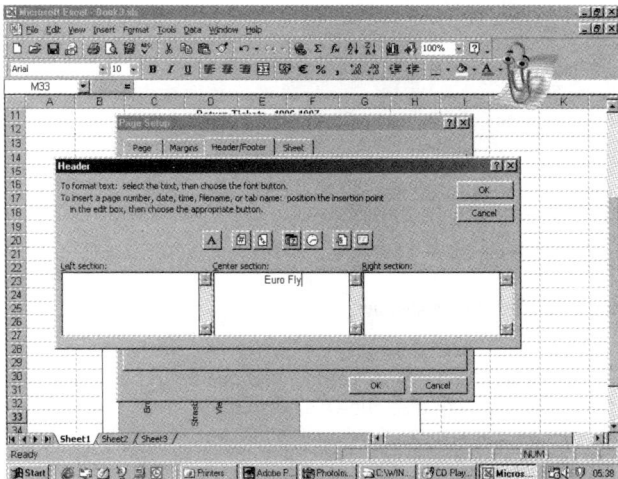

Figure 12.16 A custom header and footer.

■ Printing the worksheet

Once all the settings have been established, print your worksheet:

1. Open the File menu.

2. Select the Print option.

3. Remember to state the number of copies you wish to print.

4. If you are printing several copies, state whether you want the copies to be collated. To do this, tick the Collate box. If you do not tick it, then your copies will not be collated.

5. Confirm by clicking OK.

Printing starts.

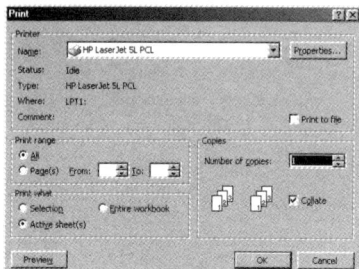

Figure 12.17 The Print dialog box.

To speed up the printing process, you can temporarily optimise the printing quality, also known as resolution. To do this, click on Properties, then on the Print Quality tab, and select the best way for printing your document. Auto is recommended because it allows the driver to decide the best print optimisation settings.

■ Selecting a different printer

If you use several printers with your computer, you can use any of them if you choose it when you go to print.

1. Open the File menu.
2. Select the Print option.
3. Click the list of printers in the Printer area.
4. Select the printer of your choice.
5. Confirm by clicking OK.

Excel and
the euro

The euro currency symbol

Currency conversion

■■

Microsoft Excel 2000 manages the new European currency, the euro, through Windows 98 which supports this sign – which can be displayed by pressing the AltGr+4 – and a complementary macro. Under Windows 95, which is not what Excel 2000 is meant to work under, you need to install the euro product update which allows the keyboard to recognise this key combination, and the euro sign font (see the Microsoft download site for more information about euro currency support for Windows 95).

■ The euro currency symbol

From 1 January 2002, when the euro becomes the sole currency for eleven countries in the EU, national currencies and the euro will have to live together. This is why it is so important to have a fast and easy to use tool. To this purpose, you need to reconfigure Windows 98 to change the default currency symbol it uses in all the applications and go straight to the euro age. These are the instructions on how to make the euro the Windows default currency, ready for the big day:

1. On the Windows desktop, click on My Computer, Control Panel, Regional Settings. Click the currency tab, the dialog box shown in Figure A.1 is then displayed.
2. Select the pound sign then press AltGr+4. The euro currency sign replaces the pound sign. Remember that the pound sign is still present in Windows. To use it, click the arrow on the left of the text box and choose it from the list.
3. Click Apply then OK.

Once the euro has been defined in Regional Settings, it is automatically included in all Windows applications. But back to Excel 2000...

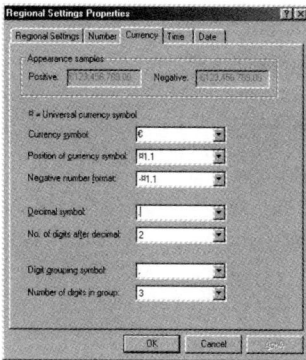

Figure A.1 This is where you define the default currency symbol in Windows.

The euro in Excel

You do not need to carry out the operation we have just described. If you are only going to use the euro in Excel, the euro can be defined in Excel in the Format Cells dialog box. The following procedure explains how to use the euro in Excel 2000.

1. Select the worksheet or the range of cells where you need to use the currency sign.

2. Click inside the selection with the right mouse button and select Format Cells (or click Format, Cells, Format Cells).

3. In the Format Cells dialog box, under the Number tab, in the Category list, select Currency.

4. Scroll the Symbol list until you find the two currency formats shown in Figure A.2.

5. Choose the symbol you wish to apply. Click OK.

The value is now expressed in euro, as shown in Figure A.3.

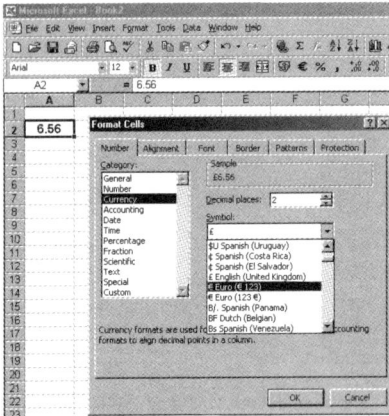

Figure A.2 Excel currency symbols propose formatting with the euro sign as a prefix or suffix.

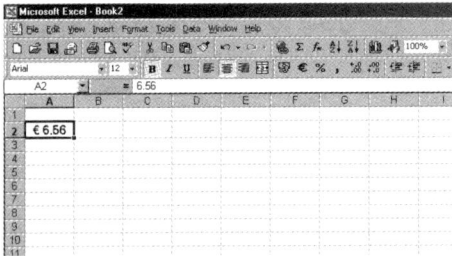

Figure A.3 The euro currency sign in Windows 98.

The euro currency sign can also be used from the Custom category. For this, choose this option in the list on the left in the Format Cells dialog box then, in the Symbol list, go down to the bottom. Select the # ##0,00 \[$e-1] formula. This has the same result as the previous operation with the advantage that you can now customise the formatting.

■ Currency conversion

During the intermediate period before definitely moving to the euro, and probably even afterwards, we will need to convert currencies into euro. The UK has not adopted the euro, so no parity was fixed. But we can take France as an example to see how this works. Parity for the French Franc was fixed on 1 January 1999 at 6.55957 to 1 euro. As in all euro conversion, this is the figure implemented in Office 2000, with the required five decimal points.

Euro Currency Tools

Excel 2000 comes with an add-in program, which provides tools (a toolbar button to format euro values and a EURO-CONVERT worksheet function) to work with euros and to convert the national currencies of the eleven countries in the euro area:

- Austria (schilling);
- Belgium (franc);
- Finland (markka);
- France (franc);
- Germany (deutschmark);
- Ireland (punt);
- Italy (lira);
- Luxembourg (franc);
- Netherlands (guilder);
- Portugal (escudo);
- Spain (peseta).

i *The following countries may adopt the euro after the initial version of EUROCONVERT, and, if so, Microsoft will update the EUROCONVERT function. For information about the new euro member currencies and updates to the EUROCONVERT function, connect to the Microsoft euro website.*

- *Denmark (krone)*
- *Greece (drachma)*
- *Sweden (krona)*
- *UK (pound sterling)*

Loading the Euro Currency Tools

The Euro Currency Tools are not loaded with Excel 2000. These are in fact add-in programs, which can be downloaded from the Microsoft website. This is the procedure for integrating the Euro Currency Tools into Excel:

1. Insert the CD-ROM for Office 2000 or for Excel 2000 in your CD drive.

2. Click Tools, Add-Ins then, in the dialog box, which is automatically displayed, tick the Euro Currency Tools check box, as shown in Figure A.4.

3. Click OK. Excel 2000 proceeds with the installation.

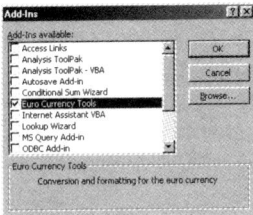

Figure A.4 Euro Currency Tools must be installed.

The formatting tool bar now has the Euro button (Figure A.5) and the EUROCONVERT worksheet function is now available.

Figure A.5 The Euro button is displayed on the formatting toolbar.

Using Euro Currency Tools

The Euro Currency Tools are now installed, and you will see how simple they are to use.

The Euro button is used to apply the euro currency style in the same way as the currency button. It assumes that you are working in euro values. However, if you are not working in euro values, then you need to use the EUROCONVERT function.

The syntax of the EUROCONVERT function looks like this:

EUROCONVERT(number,source,target,full_precision, triangulation_precision)

The *Number* is the currency value you want to convert; it can also be the reference to a cell or even the result of another function (such as SUM). *Source* refers to a three-letter abbreviation (ISO code) belonging to the home country of the currency to be converted from. *Target* is the ISO code for the currency to be converted to. The ISO codes that are accepted by the EUROCONVERT function are:

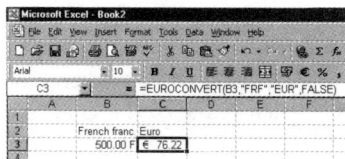

Figure A.6 The EUROCONVERT function converts the currencies for countries in the EU both into and from the euro.

Country	Currency	ISO Code
Austria	schilling	ATS
Belgium	franc	BEF
Finland	markka	FIM
France	franc	FRF
Germany	deutschmark	DEM
Ireland	punt	IEP
Italy	lira	ITL
Luxembourg	franc	LUF
Netherlands	guilder	NLG
Portugal	escudo	PTE
Spain	peseta	ESP
Euro member states	euro	EUR

Full_precision is a Boolean value (TRUE or FALSE) that specifies how the result will be rounded. If you specify FALSE then EUROCONVERT will use currency-specific rules (for example, 2 decimal places for the French Franc). If you specify TRUE then the rules are ignored and a six-digit conversion factor is used.

The last argument isn't very important unless you are using the euro as an intermediate currency between two others (for example, converting from the French Franc to the Guilder). This argument (*Triangulation_precision*) is used for rounding the intermediate euro value and has to be between 3 and 255. If you decide to omit this argument then the euro value will not be rounded.

Retrieving the result of a conversion

The next brief exercise will explain how to use the EURO-CONVERT function:

1. Click the cell that will contain the result of the conversion.

2. Click the Edit formula button at the top of the screen

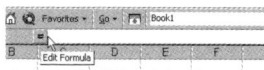

Figure A.7 The Edit formula button.

3. Click the list on the left-hand side of the Formula bar to get a choice of functions.

4. Select more functions from the drop-down list (see Figure A.8).

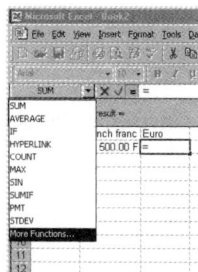

Figure A.8 The functions available.

5. You will be shown the dialog box displayed in Figure A.9. Choose User Defined, then select EUROCONVERT and click OK. Note: the number is a reference to cell B3.

6. You will then return to the Formula bar where you need to fill in the arguments (see Figure A.10).

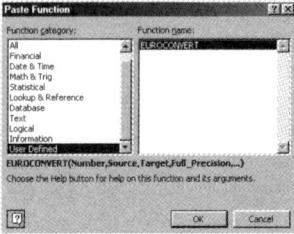

Figure A.9 Finding EUROCONVERT.

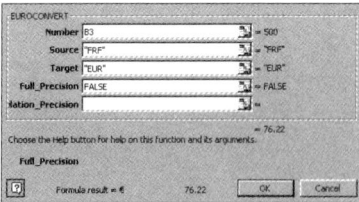

Figure A.10 EUROCONVERT has all the required calculation elements.

7. Click OK

8. Figure A.11 shows the outcome of the conversion. Please note that the cell format has been retained.

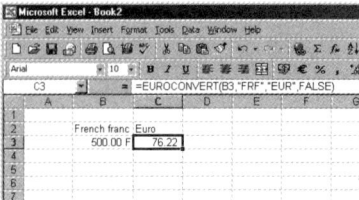

Figure A.11 EUROCONVERT places the results of its calculation in the cells which have been indicated.

Officially, EUROCONVERT will no longer be needed once the euro has become the only European currency, at least for the eleven countries that are currently part of it, but eventually possibly also for the UK, Norway and Sweden and, though it is outside the EU, for Switzerland as well. But old habits die hard – for example, the old French Franc which was used until 1 January 1960 has stayed alive in the French people's minds for over forty years, while decimalisation in the UK took a long time to be fully accepted – we can safely say that there will be people who will carry on using this very useful tool for many years to come.

Index

∎∎∎